Wonders On My Wanders

To Lesley

[signature]
05/12/12

Wonders On My Wanders

DR. DANESI SADOH PHD.

AuthorHouse™
1663 Liberty Drive
Bloomington, IN 47403
www.authorhouse.com
Phone: 1-800-839-8640

© 2012 by Dr. Danesi Sadoh PhD. All rights reserved.

No part of this book may be reproduced, stored in a retrieval system, or transmitted by any means without the written permission of the author.

First published by AuthorHouse   01/09/2012

ISBN: 978-1-4678-8276-7 (sc)
ISBN: 978-1-4678-8277-4 (hc)
ISBN: 978-1-4678-8278-1 (ebk)

Printed in the United States of America

Any people depicted in stock imagery provided by Thinkstock are models, and such images are being used for illustrative purposes only.
Certain stock imagery © Thinkstock.

This book is printed on acid-free paper.

Because of the dynamic nature of the Internet, any web addresses or links contained in this book may have changed since publication and may no longer be valid. The views expressed in this work are solely those of the author and do not necessarily reflect the views of the publisher, and the publisher hereby disclaims any responsibility for them.

Contents

Wonders On My Wanders 1
As I Wander 2
Flying The Coop 3
This Journey 4
Into The Forest 5
Ode To The Lake District 6
The English Countryside 7
Visions On My Wander 8
Ode To Love 9
Love At First Sight 10
The moment 11
Time Forgot 12
Since TheDay 13
The Look 14
I Am Your Love Convert 15
Your Love Is My Life 16
Decide My Fate 17
Irreplaceable 18
Drunk In Your Love 18
My Love Is Relentless 19
Besotted By Your Love 20
I worship In Your Love Shrine 20
Intentions For Your Love 21
Your Love My Mission 21
Loving Your Spring 22
A Blue Flame Of Love 23
Friendship Everlasting 23
My goddess, My Empress 24
My Shredded Heart 25
Your Love Keeps Me Afloat 25

Strong Boughs Of Love	26
If Love Is Your Game Plan	27
My Love Is Sold To You	28
Stairways To Your Heart	28
The Heights We Soar	29
My Darling	29
Thy Love A Musical Vision	30
Your Love Is A Sea Breeze	31
My Lamp In The Sun	31
Purveyor Of Your Dreams	32
Your Diamond In The Rough	33
You're A Blazing Sapphire	33
I Worship Your Love	34
Your Love Is Not A Cliché	35
Love Undreamed Of	36
My Love Ambrosia	37
My Angel Tis of Thee	38
A Future Heart Break	39
Juncture Of Crises	40
Oh! This Love Hurts	41
Love Without Return	42
My Love Is Lost	43
Pea From A Pod	44
My Damsel Do Not Fly	45
Storm of A Love Fight	46
Apex Of The Suns Ray	47
Passing Of A Love Storm	48
Questions About Love	49
Tidal Waves Of Destiny	50
Stinging Words	51
Tears So Fierce	52
The Tears Of Words	53

COLD HOUNDS OF LOVE	54
A SAD LAUGHTER	55
PAINFUL PASSIONS	56
A LAMENT	57
BLENDED SOUL'S OF LOVE	58
TWISTING VINES	59
THE SQUARE ROOT OF LOVE	60
RECYCLED LOVE	61
DINING ALONE	62
THIRD DEGREE BURN	63
MY LOVE NOT SO TAME	64
ODE TO JILTED LOVER	65
ODE TO A LOST SOUL	66
ODE TO A MAN BREAKER	67
A WILD RAGING FIRE	68
ODE TO OPEN MARRIAGE	69
ODE TO AYAYA'S DAUGHTER	70
ODE TO AYAYA	71
YOUR MILK OF PASSION	72
NO REGRETS FOR LOVING YOU	73
THE WAGES OF BETRAYAL	74
LOVE REFLECTIONS	75
THE FRUITS OF POISON	75
CLEANSE THY SOUL	76
LOVE ENDED TOO SOON	76
WHAT DO I TO SEE YOU AGAIN?	77
YOU VIEWED MY LOVE ASKANCE	77
LET US TAKE FLIGHT	78
ASHES OF THEIR LOVE	78
I DIED TO BE BORN AGAIN	79
THE STAINED BURROS	80
I CAN'T BELIEVE	81

IS IT THIS LOVE?	82
ELEGY TO TRUTH	83
LAUGHTER ELUDES YOU	84
PRIVILEGED PAIN	85
MY BEATING HEART	86
THE FALLING STAR	87
LOVE ON ITS HEAD	88
HER SECRET EMOTION	89
RAMBLED INTO A CRANE	90
WISHING ON A STAR	91
EPHEMERAL DAYDREAMS	92
I ONCE LOVED	93
A SMILE SO SWEET	94
A SHREDDED PAST	95
DEW DROPS	96
IF ONLY	97
TELL YOU HOW I FEEL	98
CAN YOU SEE?	99
THE EFFECTS OF OUR ACTIONS	100
HEAL THY LOVE	101
THE FUTURE OF YESTERDAY	102
CLOAK AND DAGGERS	103
SOFT CHEESE	104
REMEMBER THESE WORDS	105
THE SIGNS FROM A ROSE	106
THE ENTRAILS OF A ROSE	107
AN INGLORIOUS END	108
ENTRAPMENT	109
DREAM PERFUME	110
OPPROBRIUM	111
THIS AREN'T NO LOVE LETTER	112
GUILTY AS CHARGED	113

GUILTY OF INNOCENCE	114
PENAL SERVITUDE FOR YOUR LOVE	115
LIFE DETAINEE TO YOUR LOVE	116
DEBT OWED BE PAID!	116
DEAR LORD! I DREAM OF HOME	117
A PLACE CALLED HOME	118
YOUR WHIMSICALITY	119
A ROSE SET ME ON FIRE	120
THE CURE TO MY HEARTACHE	121
MY LOVE GATE IS OPEN	122
THE CURE FOR LOST LOVE	123
APPLICATION FOR A LOVE LOAN	124
VIRTUAL WORLD FRIEND	125
IN LOVE WITH A PIXEL	126
LOVE BY A ROMANTIC	127
LOVE CHATTER	128
TALKING LOVE	129
LOVE PARLEY	130
DREAM LOVE	130
CRAZY ENGLISH BIRD	131
ODE TO AN ENGLISH ROSE	132
MY BLOOMING ROSE	133
THE WISDOM OF THE ROSE	134
UNFOLDING OF A ROSE BUD	135
MY CRIMSON ROSE BUTTERFLY	136
LOVE WINGS LIKE A BUTTERFLY	137
BEHOLD THY BEAUTEOUS SELF	138
AHEM AHEM	139
SIMPLE PLEASURES OF YOU	140
LETS KISS	141
MY SIGNATURE OVER YOU	142
MILE HIGH CLUB	143

SOCIAL IDIOT	144
LIPSTICK ON CITY ROMANCE	145
THE DEARTH OF CHIVALRY	146
DANCING ORCHID OF A BALLERINA GIRL	147
FLIRTING WITH THE MOON	148
A BOAST OF LOVE	149
REVERSE EXHIBITIONIST	150
ODE TO THE MOON	151
ODE TO A GIRL IN RED	152
MISS MOSSY GREEN EYES	153
DOOZY ALL OVER ME	154
ODE TO MELANCHOLY	155
THE LURE OF MELANCHOLY	156
ODE TO BACCHUS	157
BETTER ME THAN THE BOOZE	158
SPRING BURST FORTH	159
REFLECTIONS	160
THE FIRST TIME WE MET	161
WHEN WE FINALLY MEET AGAIN	162
WE MEET AT LAST	163
THE PASSION OF A SCRIBE	164
VAINGLORY OF RHYMES	165
METHOD POETRY IN CHARACTER	166
LOVE PHILOSOPHY	167
OH TREE ALMIGHTY!	168
TACTLESS CRITIC	169
ODE TO A SON	170
TO A DAUGHTER	171
STROLL DOWN LOVE LANE	172
WHO WILL TELL THEM	173
DENTAL PHOBIA	174
A KNIGHT PROPOSED	175

THE KNIGHT DECIDES HIS FATE 176
A KNIGHT STATES HIS CASE 176
THE KNIGHT IMPRISONED BY LOVE 177
TESTAMENT OF THE KNIGHT 178
KNIGHT & DAMSEL (I) 179
KNIGHT & DAMSEL (II) 180
KNIGHT & DAMSEL (III) 182
KNIGHT & DAMSEL (IV) 184
KNIGHT & DAMSEL (V) 186
KNIGHT & DAMSEL (V1) 188

Wonders On My Wanders.

If I could escape from all this pressure,
hide away in a place with no tension,
in this getaway with selfish pleasure,
savour joys of a peaceful dimension.

Please let me float like an ant on a leaf,
oh currents! take me to the lock tavern,
were the wanderers imbibe in their grief,
so that I can wallow with unconcern.

I am drenched in this lingering warfare,
that life throws my way at every new turn,
for once let me deal with my own welfare,
till I can see the shoots of an upturn.

For I seek to escape by my wanders.
In the process I see so much wonders.

As I Wander

I wander endlessly without purpose,
to discover that which I do not know,
making no sense of the journey I chose,
contented to go along with the flow.

My thoughts drifting through plains of open fields,
bouncing echo against rocks so jagged,
hoping against all hope that the truth yields,
release me from falsehoods to which I'm tagged.

Yet the quest eludes me although I seek,
the morning mist melts from the suns embrace,
twists in the trail as my mind turns oblique,
hitherto clear tracks vanish without trace.

I still wander to make sense of it all.
although I stutter I refuse to fall.

Flying The Coop

Do not look for me, I have decided to elope,
into the hidden caves of my inner being,
running from the place I was a "has been",
my mind rolling down the slide of a slope.

In pursuit is the drag of my consciousness,
a dark shadow stuck in reverse projection,
across the complexion of my introspection,
now contributing to my state of restlessness.

I pause for a second to evaluate the journey,
with a throng along the road less trodden,
the veritable mass of those down trodden,
most down on their luck with no money.

Still I search deep for the right answers,
of the question I seem not to remember,
I tried hard these thoughts to dismember,
so I'm estranged from these encounters.

That is why I have chosen to fly the coop,
away from the coop, sailing on my sloop,
on this sloop, I search for lands faraway,
lands far faraway, from all these decay.

THIS JOURNEY

This arduous journey that wearies my bones,
since I embarked from the foothills of life,
away from the bounds of my comfort zones,
to seek some solace from the constant strife.

Visions of friends that fell by the way side,
and those that failed to see the crack of dawn,
the uncouth hands of hades does not time bide,
but wind swept leaves ponder across it's lawn.

How this tears rain down for the departed,
to anoint their soul for the thereafter,
sad memories of the day we parted,
pray we meet in Elysium hereafter.

Everyday life's vagaries unfolds themselves
as time pass we begin to know ourselves.

INTO THE FOREST

In the past these monuments built,
for the gods and kings of the day,
the priest invite you with their flute
come pay homage they seem to say.

From the undulating planes the crowd appeared,
to celebrate the mass of ancient and new,
forced fast of a land laid bare disappeared,
as they hold steadfast to things they knew.

The stone rock stood empty from the thrones,
and the din grew louder to the chosen hour,
a chilly sensation ran through my bones,
for despite the festivities I felt dour.

I could not lift this déjà vu feeling,
could this be a reversal into the past?
my mind kept wheeling and reeling,
I felt harassed like an actor miscast.

I knew it was time for me to run away far,
some place to get some quiet and rest,
to prevent my mind from growing a scar,
to lake district I ran into the forest.

ODE TO THE LAKE DISTRICT

The Lake district where the clouds kiss the hills,
and the foot of hills lapped by miles of lake,
I am left amazed by the wondrous thrills,
a beauty that only nature can make,
the foliage of the greenery layers thick,
wispy saplings sprinting tall as I watch,
and yellow blossoms paint the vista bright,
making the land mass slick,
no doubt the visage I see is top notch,
as I continued to enjoy the sight.

Ancient ramparts strewn across the landscape,
churches as old as the Roman advent,
the perfect place for a mind to escape,
as the peace seep away stress like a vent.
The cows here are spotted like Dalmatians,
with swans haughtier in their imperial poise,
I saw deer gather for neighbourhood watch,
lambs in celebrations,
with their joyous bleating the only noise,
as they jumped around in their wondrous patch.

The clear roads are windy as a curled snake,
white smoke from chimneys breezily bellow,
as pretty cottages in the sun bake,
yet more wonders accosted me below,
I gasped in bedazzlement at the sight,
miles and miles of rock inclines in sheer drop,
sharp dendrites pierced tendrils through rugged rocks,
overwhelmed by the might,
I finally came down from the hill top,
to be met by outlines of hotel blocks.

The English Countryside

This is a true account of the journey I just took,
doubt not, though its beyond your imagination,
I remember clearly the mysteries which I partook,
so I'm unconcerned if your head shakes in derision.

When I descended into the gorge of two valleys,
I was catapulted into a thick mist of my past,
landing like a feline in what seemed a blind alley,
as my stomach rumbled due to an absence of repast.

Around me was a scenery of the most exquisite beauty,
Nothing moved, except an ancient watermill on its rounds,
In the distance I heard a bell tinkle as if on duty,
I found myself drawn closer towards this angelic sounds.

The landscape sloped in an incline revealing greener grass,
and towards the open stood a mountain hewed from granite,
across the open field the cows faced southwards en masse,
except a bull seemingly conducting a choir out of this planet.

Out of nowhere a flock of starling birds appeared in formation,
as they reformed they signalled to me detailed information,
That told me how to watch carefully for the next predation,
so that my honour and dignity, suffer not another desecration,

Visions On My Wander

I wish you had come with me on my recent wander,
as I searched the world for anew inspiring wonder,
till I stumbled inadvertently at the garden of Eden,
my thoughts arose at what transpired in this love den.

By the shore stood a rock carved in a million years,
the shear cliff brought back memories of my fears,
as furious waves of the sea pummelled the rock face,
I was glad for the momentary respite in my life pace.

From the mountaintop I gazed at the distant mist,
Whence I saw a vision that curled my hands in a fist,
as it was revealed the difficulties that lies ahead,
and all the possibilities that ran through my head.

The waters of life are troubled that much I can say,
if we do not hearken to the voices, we will a lot pay,
the past though forgotten comes a visit in the future,
blazing through the chasm of time like a surgeons suture.

Carefully observe the wave rhythms for your own good,
Don't fail to recollect were the boulders always stood,
or you may be dashed against the rocks in a hairs breath,
if you survive you'll learn to watch for the unknown threat.

Ode To Love

Love that bounds and captures the populace,
all tongues have a word this emotion felt,
amongst the rich or poor it shows it's face,
all with a heart, has to this goddess knelt,
offering libations with no reserve,
and display proudly their sufferings gift,
cackling to the masses their good fortune,
this deity that they serve,
how illogical their minds seem to drift,
they dance merry devoid to it's mistune.

This love that feeds you with an inner strength,
that you prance around with intricate steps,
as you enjoy these carefree times at length,
the pleasured rush unconcerned by missteps,
floating with joy on the magic carpet,
a blissful chapter with not enough time,
for this great feeling has captured your being,
you are now a limpet,
and may fail to hear the song is a mime,
though with eyes, you no longer are seeing.

Oh love! that shines like a light in the night,
from the bottom pit takes over the soul,
powered by the secrets of kryptonite,
energy that lifts you from the black hole,
this same feeling so painful when it ends,
entrapped in it's lure you try to reach out,
you ask for more as a yawn they smother,
rebuffed like love offends,
you the devout they now wish to block out,
love dead will be born afresh another.

LOVE AT FIRST SIGHT

Do you believe that loves at first sight truly exist?
A mere glance and you are eternally enamoured,
although the enchantress lips you have still not kissed,
their attention you feel is all you ever clamoured.

With your senses you grapple, but your thoughts are suffused,
For you thirst for them, like a plant needs photosynthesis,
and you feel without their light your mood is confused,
they are now the oxygen that breaks down your love synthesis.

Now you swagger with a nonchalance chanting their name,
and your being lightened as a feather, is afloat in the breeze.
So you whisper to the whole world that this is your dame,
She is more adorable than all the worlds love fairies.

You never stopped to think if your love was reciprocated,
because it never crossed your mind it will not be returned,
you did not check carefully if the damsel has assented,
thinking that something this strong cannot be spurned.

My friend do not despair this is the nature that love takes,
to separate you from the deadly tentacles of the fakes,
though your heart suffers deeply from the love shakes,
you will derive a valuable lesson from your mistakes.

THE MOMENT

The moment I set my eyes on you,
I just knew there was something,
ticking in tandem between us,
mayhap, you felt the chemistry too.
You know, that underlying oomph factor,
which sometimes flows like a lake
of liquid love going away downstream,
carrying with it all of our dreams,
the hopes and sometimes aspirations,
those with whom we yearn to be ours.
My inner essence swam with the tide,
easy strokes towards your heart centre,
Transported to the blissful fort of utopia
and fortified by a wall of mutual reciprocity.
Definitely, I seem to perceive that you
are onto me the way I am surely onto you.
Just waiting for the moment that will
break the ice so cause you to fall right onto,
my eager waiting arms, which will enfold you.
Till then, I imagine the nature that is your love.

TIME FORGOT.

Right at the gates of love we sealed a kiss,
watching a hungry cloud eat up the moon,
as we enjoyed the scenery in bliss,
we both could have stayed put until high noon.

Our hearts raced with joy down the mountain slopes,
exploring rages of a rough terrain,
landing with a thump could not dash out hopes,
neither spoilt by signs of a summer rain.

Time stood still as we wondered what it meant,
hoping the solitude last a life time,
of natures peerless beauty heaven sent,
disturbed by the brusqueness of human mime.

We lay languid at the peak of the rock.
Time forgot to move the hands of the clock.

Since The Day

How so much time has eloped since the day,
things are no longer the same anymore,
the lucky survivors are left to pay,
for the aftermath of a needless war.

See! they fought so hard because they believed,
assailed by the loud clamour for vengeance,
never thought they were there to be deceived,
the faith of the motherland in defence.

They told them it was okay to slaughter,
the blood of the enemy was not real,
with that in mind doubtless they will falter,
kill with impunity then have a meal.

Lost in the innocence of tomorrow,
they forgot they had to face their sorrow.

THE LOOK

The look you gave me in the train sent my heart a flutter
But I was too shy to say hello in case I got the wrong signal
Don't want everyone looking and thinking who is this nutter

When I composed myself to speak with you I had to stutter
Twas embarrassing that my nerve completely failed me, though
The look you gave me in the train sent my heart a flutter

Your kindness to my failure's made my being melt like butter
At that moment I wanted to express my feeling to you, but
Don't want everyone looking and thinking who is this nutter

Will try again and be careful with the words that I utter
I Just need to think how to break the ice for you to know
The look you gave me in the train sent my heart a flutter

Hell, who cares what anyone thinks I should just mutter
Something very discreet for your ears only because I
Don't want everyone looking and thinking who is this nutter

Now I got to take the bull by the horn and hope not to sputter
Maybe the right moment when no on is looking I should say
The look you gave me in the train sent my heart a flutter
Don't want everyone looking and thinking who is this nutter

I Am Your Love Convert.

Tremulous waves prevails across my spine,
a shot through the aperture of my soul,
as my star collapsed into a black hole,
having lost the brightness of its shine.

Your love calms the tempest of a stormy sea,
and steadies the ill winds that rock the boat,
you're my guardian angel that keeps me afloat,
from all the deep troubles from which I flee.

So I berth at the sturdy pilings of your dock,
seeking shelter from the squall of dark clouds,
an encampment of refuge far from the crowds,
which always opens to me whenever I knock.

Your sereneness mollifies my impetuosity for you,
availed by the poise of your temperate nature,
you protect me from the glare of overexposure,
an inestimable liaison from my angle of view.

To try putting a value of your worth to me,
like counting the grains of sand in a desert,
is hopeless to measure to an adequate degree,
let me just simply say I'm your love convert.

Your Love Is My Life

You dance the strange love of a praying mantis,
and strike a tone like red summer lipstick,
a flame flickers at the tip of your wick,
an afterglow that lights up Atlantis.

Your soft fragrance teases my wild senses,
and ruffles the angst out of my feathers,
till calm pervades like monastic cloisters,
the burning heat in me slowly eases.

Treacle me blind with your sweet molasses,
let me taste the flavour of your syrup,
pour me a large measure on my love cup,
until you satiate all my impulses.

Your love remains the nexus of my life.
Without your love I lack the taste for life.

DECIDE MY FATE

I am not rich but you make me wealthy,
though with no clothes you hide my nakedness,
you protect me and keep me healthy,
and hide me from this world of wickedness,

You unravel my doubts like a mystic,
provide answers to rival Solomon,
your vision for me is futuristic,
and keeps me from the influence of mammon.

You who commands be and so it will be,
a conviction that beguiled the faithless,
but with the power of your words set free,
to fulfil the righteous and the doubtless.

In your dominion I have placed my faith.
It is your will that shall decide my fate.

Irreplaceable

From the foliage of a bloom you appeared,
borne on the crown of a long fine stamen,
with your décolletage smudged in blood red,
a view that sets the heart aflame of men.

You curled up close to the warmth of my heart,
but your love faded in the setting sun,
and it pained me much to see you depart,
I hope you will be back in the long run.

Winds of my love blows in your direction,
cooling the moisture in your feverish soul,
as steam dissipating all disaffection,
ridding you of the shadow of the ghoul.

Your loving me may be replaceable,
but my sweet love is irreplaceable

Drunk In Your Love

Do I appear in your dreams at night,
drunk from tasting the brandy on your lips,
then try to take off like a kite in flight,
although you still wish me to have more sips.

The evergreen of my trailing arbutus,
brings to you calmness from the scorching heat,
the sap of it's fruit provides you victus,
and soft cream to soften your supple feet.

Yet your searching words brings tears to my eyes,
drops roll along my eyelids and are stuck,
I try hard this blinding pain to disguise,
but it hits me like I'm by lightening struck.

If it's your will, my love is yours to have,
"pari passu" do not your loving halve.

My Love Is Relentless

You glow in the glare of a day so young,
repelled by the coarseness of calloused hands,
because to you the spring only just sprung,
you are not yet ready for life's demands?

When your gleam mellows in the dawn of night,
then into the twilight your suitors melt,
and the false knights have all taken their flight,
will ye wonder why this fate was to you dealt?

As crows feet indent it's cruel marks on time,
the glory of past but a memory,
though you cling on to the slime of your prime,
all that you used to be is now history?

The gushing of the river is endless.
Though time changes my love is relentless.

Besotted By Your Love.

Besotted! Since my eyes on you befell,
you are to me, an oasis of calm;
I fell deep into your amorous spell,
enthused by the coolness of your aplomb.

You voice seem echoed by the whistling pine,
when your wispy twigs call out my name,
in a pitch tasty as sweet melon vine,
which only serves to my deep desire inflame.

Your aquifer replenishes my soul,
with the convivial fruits of unity;
I drink deeply from your watering hole,
and bask in the joy of this amity.

I am tightly entwined in your love zone.
Your affection hits me like a cyclone.

I worship In Your Love Shrine.

If I was certain of your love one day,
your undivided attention and care,
and I know it's not just a mystery play,
or a wicked way my soul to ensnare.

I will vanquish the most evil demon,
conquer the battle across the ages,
show you my loyalty is uncommon,
till we're part of the folklore of sages.

In a desert breeding bland saxual trees
only your stalk display a rare spring Rose,
succulent petals fresh as a sea breeze,
although the mirage of a sandstorm blows.

I'm in deep freeze until your love is mine.
On my knees I will worship in your shrine.

Intentions For Your Love

If I can coax your love out of it's lair,
so you see from my eyes a bright sunshine,
and I blaze through you like a solar flare,
till your hue becomes deeper than blush wine.

I'll float you on a bed of clouds gently,
then vulcanise your essence towards me,
show the extent of my love intently,
pure feelings you have no choice but to see.

My queen bee to whom I'm in servitude,
let me produce nectar for your honey,
show my loyalty with a certitude,
you want to become my sexy bunny.

I now surrender to your intentions.
You can see that I have no pretensions.

Your Love My Mission

It's you I think of at the crack of dawn,
the last vision I see before my sleep,
your plumage imperial as a white swan,
a flawless jewel that grown men will weep.

I hear your voice in a nightingales song,
your eyes sparkling like raindrops in a pearl,
and fragrance permeating the air night long,
to me you represent the perfect girl.

Your love cuts deep like a cleaver through straw,
though a sheaf of grain I'll rather be yours,
to bow deeply to your loving in awe,
and if it's your wish I'll fall on all fours.

This is the testament of my passion.
To capture your love is now my mission.

Loving Your Spring

The first evidence of a brand new spring,
and your sweet love is as fresh as a daisy,
blown by the wind of change to an upswing,
the imbued affection sends me crazy.

Knowing you care lifts me to the precipice,
and your good loving floats me heaven high,
I feel I have found my life's accomplice,
someone with whom I can see eye to eye.

The force of your love sprouts the daffodils,
and tulips to display enchanting hues,
a splendid scene that is most ideal,
for our loving to abound and suffuse.

Your love to me is deep and abiding,
and the way we feel is coinciding.

A Blue Flame Of Love

The mere thought of you ignites a blue flame,
lights even the darkest parts of my soul,
like a new season of chances just came,
convince new wings of passion to sprout whole,
my spirits lifted high by your command,
with new purpose I face the coming strife,
knowing you will be there to hold my hands,
gently guide me through the rough winds of life.
with twinkly eyes brighter than a new star,
smile that lifts the gloom of this winters day,
your soft lips sweeter than a bees nectar,
mellow voice calm as a musical play.
for with you my heart shall be whole again.
with you my love sack will be filled with grain.

Friendship Everlasting

From my mind eye I observed your sweet soul,
you sprout like buds of an hibiscus plant,
in florescence when my good words cajole,
petals bloom in glory to my love chant
I cherish a friendship everlasting,
stubborn than a mule with a bone to pick,
that weathers the roughest sea outlasting,
just like a pair of proud love Swans we click,

We will be challenged by the test of time,
that will tell if we have affinity,
at the critical hour the clock shall chime,
to tell if this last to infinity.

Lets be proud in each other's company.
Lets hope that our bond accompany.

My Goddess, My Empress

The moment I set my eyes on your face,
my mind drew a beautiful love portrait,
remindful of a scene on a Ming vase,
both of us posing in a self-portrait.

The golden sunshine rises with your smile,
sets when your face squeezes into a frown,
and the bloom of orchids copies your style,
wilt offseason, while you never break down.

You are my most tasty cream parfait,
layered with sweet dollops of fresh goodies,
I look forth to your flavour every day,
nothing taste as good as your blueberries.

I worship your love, my divine goddess,
let me be at your service, my empress.

My Shredded Heart

What's in thou that I a cuckolded, pine?
Thy virtue exposed to a passing wind,
that you wished to delete my past with thine,
and the life we hath built thou had all binned.

That neither my loss of honour nor shame,
amongst my own peers to whom I'm debased,
because I had thought thy where a real dame,
right up to when thou rendered me abased,

Thou art floundered thy love like a ship wreck,
with the bulk of it's hulk dashed against rocks,
till signs of life was extinct at the deck,
devastation wrought by too many shocks.

Thou hath shredded my heart into mince meat,
but my heart beats for thou through thy deceit.

Your Love Keeps Me Afloat

The things important to me in this life,
will pale to nothingness if you left me,
my life will spin into a bitter strife,
for it is you who holds the master key.

Without you the air is sucked from my lungs,
I need you to calm the rages of ages,
with the smooth assurance of your silk tongue,
guiding my soul gently through the stages.

For when I gaze at your limpid blue eyes,
I dive for diamonds in the deep blue sea,
your heart inside a solitaire disguise,
and I through the sparkles a future see.

You are the string that keeps my flag afloat.
You are the buoyancy with which I float.

STRONG BOUGHS OF LOVE

My love remains sturdy as an oaks trunk,
rooted in place come severe wind or storm,
surviving what ever comes on pure spunk,
my true love for you will never transform.

To your whims my boughs so strong bends across,
in hope to feel the lattice of your thoughts,
but the depth of your mind leaves me at loss,
though my branchlets can resist the wind burst.

Askance at my weather beaten carcass,
you fail to see the life that stirs within,
shame your outlook is through a tinted glass,
for my sins, I must take it on the chin.

My deep love is as stubborn as a mule.
I hope you never take me for a fool.

If Love Is Your Game Plan

Despite all said and done your love beckon,
like cheese on a mousetrap in a corn field,
it's worthwhile to face the peril, I reckon,
for to your adore I have wish to yield.

Your allure supersedes my self-control,
and to overcome your wiles I've not planned,
rather I desire as your muse enrol,
to be at your good service and command.

Whenest the shrill notes from your clarion call,
I mount my destrier ready for the joust,
for I fear not on your behest to brawl,
as long as its on me your love is doused.

To you I am your most humble liegeman.
I stand ready to fulfil your game plan.

My Love Is Sold To You

Even though it's to you my love is sold,
like petrels in flight you're elusive,
whilst heaven high my virtues you extolled,
hopes of repast with you are illusive.

You remain steadfast in your habitat,
loath to explore blood vessels in my heart,
my pulse rate fluctuates down a tortuous path,
till I feel my poor pump will break apart.

My soul exposed to you as a clean slate,
for the stylus of your fervour to scrawl,
and append the nature of your heart rate,
for it is to you I am held in thrall.

Take a leap of faith into my bastion,
Let me shower you with adulation.

Stairways To Your Heart

Could I ever ascend the stairways to your mind?
Carted unto the opulence of your essence,
so I taste the purest form of your quintessence,
An exclusive part of you, I wish to have mined.

How is it to my sincere love you are so blind?
To my adore you respond with evanescence,
although I wish to be with you till senescence,
sweet love if only you are not so disinclined.

For your providence I wish to toil from the earth,
provide to you an abundance for your table,
and be a true guardian as long as I draw breath.

Do not doubt the truth I speak for I am able,
our love bonded will be a spiritual rebirth,
let the groundswell of this affection enable

THE HEIGHTS WE SOAR

When I'm sad its to you I seek succour,
for I find you alone can comfort me,
as you paint my mood in water colour,
and wash my sadness into the deep sea.

My heavy heart is lightened with your words,
that touches the core of my soul stable,
an assuring music with the right chords,
takes control of me till I am able.

You change my weather from winter to spring,
Fountain of life emerge from my inner self,
instantly my look is on the upswing,
and I have a renewed pride in myself.

Your wings lift my soul to the highest clouds.
From your shoulders I peer above the crowds.

MY DARLING

For my darling I yearn most earnestly,
pining with hunger for when we shall meet,
to her image my thought returns constantly,
with a smile as fresh as the winter sweet.

I hanker to taste from her luscious lips,
and feel the tremble of her angel heart,
as my hands perch gingerly on her hips,
whisper to her we shall not again part.

Like a diaphanous veil, I sense her mind,
which tells a story of eternal love,
and for which our destiny is entwined,
an underwritten statement of true love.

This is the signature of my adore.
For it is your world that I now implore.

Thy Love A Musical Vision

Your thoughts provokes a musical vision,
winds sway green leaves in balletic whispers,
and invokes a sandstorm of intentions
yet my love burrows deep in blind bunkers

Your mind is like a pretty rose flower,
lusty but your thorns pricks the emotion,
but changing moods do not my heart turn sour,
rough winds will one day calm in the ocean.

Love does not disappear without reason,
If I wronged you then show your forgiveness,
though you feel I committed high treason,
I will now surely address my weakness.

Time procures the healing of heartbreak.
In time my heart will come forth from the wreck.

Your Love Is A Sea Breeze

Your eyes transmit expressions of my hopes,
faster than a kayak racing downstream,
a good feeling that makes me want to scream,
as my mind races your thoughts down the slopes.

Let me paddle your stern with sliding strokes,
so my rocker stops you from capsizing,
that in the rough seas it's to me you cling,
to calmly from the crest of the wave coax.

You float me like a pollen in the breeze,
shooting an avalanche of fizz through me,
till I want to go on a loving spree,
just to calm the scorching flames of your tease.

You keep me from drowning in the deep seas.
You refresh me like an evening sea breeze.

My Lamp In The Sun

You're a luminescent lamp in the sun,
burning flaming red like the desert heat,
that my Tongue is parched from your scorching fun,
slaked by the love burn of your whiskey neat.

You incite my vibes with your translucence,
shimmering in the bay of a lagoon,
I bask in the glow of the candescence,
until becoming overwhelmed I swoon.

Spark the full flavour of my energy,
indulge in the ambience of my relish,
we will sync in a timeless synergy,
if you release my craving from the leash

My heart is festooned with the heat of love,
I hope you drape me with the loops of love.

PURVEYOR OF YOUR DREAMS

I will not pretend to be your champion,
but rather let me be at your service,
call me whenever you need some action,
and you will perceive I'm not a novice.

If it is your wish I'll crawl like an ant,
to partake in the feast of two mountains,
and when sated I will your love name chant,
about the springs that flows from your fountains.

Flow in the current of my filament,
don't resist the torsion of my ballast,
instead augment my ferment with your scent,
and together we will be one at last.

Let me be the purveyor of your dreams,
Swing into my life and fulfil my dreams.

Your Diamond In The Rough

Can I be your diamond in the rough?
in your hands turn into a sparkly gem,
that your care has uncovered from the raw,
as a virtue of your planned stratagem.

Will you polish my stones with your smooth wax?
till I reflect my qualities in full,
so that in your love finger I relax,
satisfy your desire to the brimful.

Show me the ladder to your love window,
grant me the keys for exclusive entrance,
and I will in your secret canoe row,
until I rock your boat into my trance.

Let me dwell in the confines of your zone.
I will mine your quarry for my gemstone.

You're A Blazing Sapphire

You light the skies like a blazing sapphire,
ascending into the clouds on a star,
as if a comet has set you on fire,
and caused the heavens to rain down nectar.

Let me plunge into your solar system,
exhaust my volatiles in your meteor,
so that I'm part of your ecosystem,
savouring in enthralment your allure.

Kindle my coal till it burns a fever,
and the vapours of steam, baths me in sweat,
that in shivers I turn a believer,
and you cool me with a sponge soaking wet.

Let me feel the force of your solar flare,
You shine with glare of a maiden so fair.

I Worship Your Love

I worship your indelible beauty,
and abase myself in supplication,
to serve your needs is my filial duty,
for you bring me waves of satisfaction.

Your smile reveals glimpses of paradise,
revives and redeems my worthless spirit,
my deep love for you is my only vice,
and to your magnificence I submit.

You empower me in your graciousness,
and transform my love to heavenly tides,
I'm overwhelmed by your amativeness,
when in the moonless waters my oars glides.

My heart beats to the music of your breath,
without you I have not long on this earth.

Your Love Is Not A Cliché

If I knew how to write love poetry,
I will scroll you an ode so beatific,
with words that show, you're terrific,
trying to explain to all, your coquetry.

I will not insult you with a common cliché,
comparing you to the sun, moon or a star,
neither will I claim you're a super star,
or cleverly describe you as my love odyssey.

I'll not write, without you my life will end,
or claim to see you in the petals of a Rose,
as you sashay in the wind, then strike a pose,
like Elizabeth Taylor a film legend.

No I will be much more stylised than that,
use similes that escaped the bards of old,
like something that can cure the common cold,
and it will come to me at the drop of a hat.

Sadly I have no clue about love poetry,
neither am I versed in language sorcery
so you are the moon the sun and the star
and while I'm here you're my superstar.

Love Undreamed Of

If I trace for you the arc of a rainbow,
will you curve your love towards me,
let the tendrils of your vines embrace me,
so we reach across the sky to a moon bow.

Let me separate the richness of your colours,
so I can distil the purity of your essence,
and perceive the fullness of your ambience,
to lift me out of the grip of the vapours.

Your love transcends the heavens above,
even the cloud blushes blue in your homage,
so the sun could catch a view of your image,
to see a phenomenon previously undreamed of.

Wish you could tuck me into your flower bud,
then unfold me so the world see you're mine,
watching in wonder as our lives intertwine,
and disavow their mind that this is a dud.

Let's wade through the thicket of the brush,
trim the rough edges smooth till it's lush,
so the long path of our love becomes clear,
and together we discover a new frontier.

My Love Ambrosia

You washed my pain in the shadows of rain,
soaked me in fluids of tender love and care,
and eased my strain into a paddling drain,
until I was ready my soul to bare.

Your sweet ambrosia is my elixir,
that on my heart causes a joyful spring,
inebriated by juice in your mixer,
that I flow in the rhythm of your swing.

Let me feel the full depth of your knowledge,
reveal to me secrets of your garden.
that leaves me no doubt but to acknowledge,
that yours was from the apple of Eden.

Your love diffused the tension in my heart,
with your love I found the beat of my heart

My Angel Tis of Thee

In my heart was settled a sparrow,
which for a brief visit built a nest,
and it came to know my sorrow,
it subsumed to become my guest.

Therefore to my angel tis of thee,
The sustenance that feed my being,
For thy incomparable soul so trustee,
Lighting the flame of this feeling.

I sing your praise the most high,
Let the wind whisper round the world,
spread your name like seeds of wild rye,
So that your banner might be unfurled.

It is to your loving arms I surrender,
To seek succour from the vipers spit,
basking in the warmth of your splendour,
and to your loyalty I forever commit.

Let not the swell of emotion gather any moss,
Let it be that the bond shall be unbreakable,
Let us share together the burden of the cross,
Let for us the nature of our love be unmistakable.

A Future Heart Break.

One day you will break my lonely heart,
Don't ask how I came to know about this,
I just know it will surely be torn apart,
though you reassure me with a candy kiss.

The cloud is pregnant with these questions,
like what kind of love will come raining,
to dilute the strength of my suggestions,
and keep my delicate mind from draining.

The right answers to these are most fuzzy,
for although the sun shines brightly today,
the pathway to the future is still muzzy,
so I reveal my concerns in a heart felt way.

Is there a chance this is the real thing,
that what we feel now, will last forever,
and not just dissipate as in a fast fling,
which doesn't have deep feelings whatsoever.

Well, maybe I am just a sentimental old fool,
who still believes falling in love is cool,
for indeed you are my sole inspirational fuel,
so I beg you, stand by me and do not be cruel

Juncture Of Crises

Do you have in you a wish to emasculate me,
by shrinking my "bullous Grandes" to peanut,
and turn me into your very own effeminate man,
like a eunuch in the court of Queen Elizabeth?

If only you knew the things my eyes have seen,
I wonder if you know what my ears have heard,
wishing you are aware the lashings on my soul,
before our path crossed in the juncture of crises?

With my own eyes I saw a sheep devour a lion,
A gentle cat barked with a voice of thunder,
my soul was scalded by the wrath of lightening,
as I walked through the streets of trepidation.

Wrestled not with Medusa in the theatre of battles,
an epic struggle that almost sapped my life force,
that I stumbled fearing my demise has arrived,
to succumb to your whimsical and capricious nature.

So put a brake on it and let me continue my wander,
like a Shepherd leading a flock of sheep to water,
searching for new pastures for them to succour,
this is the new warrior head I have now become

OH! THIS LOVE HURTS

Why is it that though love hurts the mind much?
My heart still desire to your love ache for,
pleading you heal it with your tender touch,
it beats harsh to your emotions implore.

Whereas the thought of you stings like a wasp,
worse will it be if your hand I don't win,
that in dolour the faintest hope I grasp,
on my knees pray for forgiveness of sin.

It is you who gives candy it's sweet taste,
that I'm now an addict with a sweet tooth,
thirsting for your honey that is love laced,
so to be quenched by the bloom of your youth.

Glad to suffer if love comes from this pain.
Hope you know my love will never wane.

Love Without Return

If I possessed wings, will I fly away,
whenever the season is unfavourable,
and like father Christmas in a sleigh,
distribute my presents, so its acceptable.

Do I fight for love or maybe flight for love?
I cannot delete my thoughts like a computer,
for it encamps my mind like a metal glove,
sticking close to me in the way of a suitor.

Can I love you without expecting a return?
Worship the ground you walk on from afar,
though whenever I remember my heartburn,
as if the sky is scalded by a shooting star.

To the new life you live, will I look askance?
Now I am no longer the centre of your gravity,
hoping against hope, you miss me too perchance,
or could this be just a symptom of my depravity.

The answers to these questions I do not know,
as my thought processes seem to download slow,
maybe you can help me, in my quest to forego,
So I can finally depart from the status quo.

My Love Is Lost

I cannot find where I left my love,
could I have lost it in your heart,
I've searched all lands and the sky above,
maybe a wizard stole it by black art?

This love is full of laughter and good mood
in the dullest winter brings a glow,
and warms the spirit up like good food,
to misplace it, is to me a big blow.

I miss the way this love made me smile,
even when cars splash puddles on me,
this love would stop me from been hostile,
quelling my angst like magic potpourri.

A large reward awaits anyone who finds it,
tell love my heart aches to meet once again,
my candle of desire is eternally lit,
I need it to come and quench my pain.

This love be it in the wide seas or hill tops
in the high clouds or ocean depth,
or hiding in the folds of tear drops,
shall not escape me till I'm out of breath.

Pea From A Pod

You took me away from me
Left me with an empty shell
Shed like the pea from a pod
Landed in unfamiliar shores
Searching for a new identity
Trying to germinate new roots
But the soil around is infertile
So the sorry sight of my saplings
No good even for the cow graze
My neighbours are sturdy weeds
Who revels in this toxic environ
I suffocate as faster they grow
The tiny nutrient they suck away
I shrivel everyday that comes anew
Not sure what my future will hold
But sure as the rising of the sun
The vicissitudes of night and day
I shall be here to see tomorrow
Most exceedingly, your liege-man

My Damsel Do Not Fly

My damselfly so captivating its your praise I write,
I remember when you first captured my attention,
the day you buzzed my ear and gave me a mighty fright,
caused me to flip back in shock with a hypertension.

Now I stroll down the coastal and estuarine marshes,
looking to catch a sight of your graceful stylish form,
with an ease of motion you settle on the grove branches,
sometimes masses of your friends cluster in a swarm.

Your delicate figure brings out my chivalrous nature,
I stand ready to rescue you from any danger my damsel,
when your extensive pruinescence brings out your allure,
I do feel embarrassed by the scruffiness of my flannel.

Watching you rest and sun yourself by the waterside,
gives me a feeling of satisfaction never before felt,
sometimes my affection overwhelms me that I cried.
Truly, I know what I feel for you must be heartfelt.

So my dearest Damsel do not from my love fly away,
the love which is as straight as the apian way,
and the day my love is returned I will shout hooray,
hoping that this hour comes soon without delay.

STORM OF A LOVE FIGHT

Drifting snow swirls across the wind surface,
signalling an outpouring of deep emotion felt,
as dark shades of past angst fitfully resurface,
around the atmosphere a cumuliform cloud dwelt.

It used to be that love was with us resident,
remember when we both of summers return dreamt,
stargazing with the periscope of eager adolescent,
till a serpent with the apple of your desire tempt.

A bite of the poison transmogrified your affection,
Into a monster that sought to devour my entrails,
disseminating hatred like an opportunistic infection,
behind left clumps of destruction in your coattails.

Herein remains the aftermath of a scorched earth policy,
after all this you wish me to help rebuild the edifice,
hey presto, you make me the focus of your exit policy,
as you present me the emaciated frame of an armistice.

Why must it be that heads you win and tail I lose?
Betting it has not crossed your mind I can refuse,
even though you have done things to me that are taboos,
alright, let me think about things after I take a snooze.

Apex Of The Suns Ray

Hey my friends, let me bestow on you a tale,
look at me now attired in rags and all bones,
I used to be the lord of my own fairy tale,
till buffeted with forces of mighty cyclones.

You do not believe I commanded vast armies,
owned palaces across the plains of Nirvana,
from all side I was the envy of my enemies,
as lictors fawned over me like a prima donna.

Now you wondering how come I am now so poorly,
It was my queen who betrayed my secrets,
opened up my guards to a cuckold so cleverly,
to unravel the codes of my sanctum by billets.

Do not look so piteously at my lugubrious face,
the seeds of my glory shall sprout once more,
although impecunious I am in a higher place,
so save your tears for there's nothing to cry for.

The good lord said Vengeance is mine I shall repay,
don't you know comeuppance arrives on judgement day?
As I speak the centre of their camp is in disarray,
while am at peace walking by the apex of the suns ray.

Passing Of A Love Storm

A Dream State Of Love
Reposing on a bench watching the world drift along,
I embarked on a journey into gloomy introspection.
A bolt of light flashed a sense of right & wrong,
why do ants walk in a straight line, my reflection.

Anything could I have done to make a difference?
Perchance straighten the arc of a rainbow, like wise,
reposition the emblems to restore your new balance,
even as you intensely gaze at me with snaky eyes.

Everything be known about affection I have endeavoured.
Thought the circlet of commitment signify love eternal,
but with spite and noisome my rapprochement bespattered,
And gingerly at first I committed to write this journal.

Do you gaze at the sky as the winds changes direction?
Watch cumulus clouds marking out prints of your future,
proselytising for the answers to your mental rejection,
despising verisimilitude's that causes you discomfiture.

Flickers of rapid eye movement synchronised I start to shake,
the ground opens its bowels to swallow me as if in a quake,
It cannot be real that everything you did for me was a fake.
Agasp! I bolt upright in sweat, dreaming I must be awake.

Questions About Love

Were does love elope to when its no longer?
Does it basically retire to a distant island,
to whence it recuperates to resolve its anger,
defeating all entreaties by mounting a highland?

Do you remember when the feeling was glowing?
That everything about them, so pulchritudinous,
even finding the tedium of their screed flowing,
and for their hunger, you mind not be abstemious.

Twas us made plans to conquer all in our vista,
opened up our soul, so you could stare deep down,
and our spate not encompass able in the AltaVista,
the affection so deep we're the talk of the town.

Never in our thought process did we think of an end,
until the end got our thought process to do a think.
So here we are on the bend, as we cannot comprehend,
what it was in retrospect, that was the missing link.

Tarry awhile; let me ponder this rhetorical question.
Do not harry me for answers, with your pontification.
I will let you know, when I come up with my solution.
Till then, please don't accuse me of any obfuscation

Tidal Waves Of Destiny

I feel the tidal wave of destiny wash over me,
with my feet I shall surf the swell to glory,
though winds may blow across the tempestuous sea,
my determination is not to end as a sob story.

I know my life journey will not be a linear graph,
it will be mired with curves and unexpected twists,
along the way It is clear I will make a gaffe,
for this is what the totem of a span consists.

Although I stumble I will surely rise again,
next time I will know were the trip wire lies,
any similar life traps will be set in vain,
for they will not be the cause of my demise.

It's sheer idiocy to anticipate a smooth sailing ride,
then stand agape when a mishap comes along the way,
failing to tackle the weight of the rising tide,
watching helplessly as your aspirations trifle away.

Preparation is the bullet proof of the unexpected,
the things you have done before are interconnected,
your previous hard work will render you protected,
so no matter the shots you will be resurrected.

Stinging Words

Your words stung as the crack of a whip,
although the hide of my skin is thick,
the constant excoriation made me sick,
that is the reason you see me as I weep.

My sadness melts ice from a glacier,
water flooding the face of the rock,
I retreat to highlands as you mock,
the sounds of taunts become bawdier.

How love has incurred a great debt,
the price of loyalty an expensive gift,
all my gestures to you getting short shrift,
playing mind games like Russian roulette.

The moon cantered over to the sun,
till it felt the harsh glare of it's stare,
I was awash in the shower of your flare,
but never was it a basket load of fun.

Love was leveraged against emotion,
to test the deep nature of my devotion,
but alas this time it was just too much,
you forced me to be covered in mulch

TEARS SO FIERCE

On the precipice loosely hangs a single tear,
failing to roll down a trail on my cheek,
as the darkness descends in a night so bleak,
I fight with the mixed emotions of my fear.

Sad this affair has thus taken a tortuous path,
do remember the time this love was so fresh,
spring water gushing from waterfall afresh,
soaked deep in the pleasures of a bubble bath.

I hold back this tears from tracking a trail,
limpid balls gliding smoothly in locomotion,
must meander away from this express emotion,
though a strong gale beckons I put on a veil.

Caught in the vortex of a continuous whirlwind,
spinning around in the funnel of its dust cloud,
wrapped tightly in the embrasure of a shroud,
struggling that my mind is not blown downwind.

I must resist the lure of this tears so fierce,
though pained by pricks in my heart that pierce,
within to withal the day will break with light,
I am suspended from the mist that is my blight.

THE TEARS OF WORDS

Listen, no copious penning of rhymes,
swirling like black smoke from wood fire,
versed in intricate words that inspire,
can excavate the deep decay of love crimes.

No matter how sonorous the words chimes,
how great the rhythm of the stanza flow,
no matter the positive critiques that glow,
cannot replace, O' my love of lost times.

I'd rather be loved by someone than of it write,
this habit that helps to assuage the pain,
the outpouring that helps to keep me sane,
till the time comes that shines a love light.

So if the words prance like a chivalrous knight,
with a swash buckle style slay the monster,
this abstract action is all the words can muster,
lonely is the side of the bed in the dead of night.

These words though sweet mask the tears,
Between the lines lies the key to many fears,
the sleeve to the deep core worn inside out,
left to you to discover what this is all about.

Cold Hounds Of Love

Some consider love a fair game for deception,
a competition to play, with not a fair rule,
they infiltrate your mind by means of inception,
switching on to tourney mode as you start to drool

These cold hounds will crash into your crush,
then crush you watching in delight as you crash,
playing with your emotions till you're mush,
sticking to their iniquities like a bad rash.

Baying out loud for a taste of your blood,
excited by smell of prey in the prevailing wind,
wishing to drag your carcass through the mud,
they operate stealthily so keep your eyes skinned.

Your Maidens blush has blossomed into a cactus,
spines prickle you to shed rivers of tears,
how sorrowful you're for your waning status,
at this development that caught you unawares.

In the quest for love be ready for betrayal,
Opening your heart but guarding it with care.
All the Jezebel's prowling for victims, beware,
you have giving love a most deformed portrayal.

A Sad Laughter

Just because you now hear my loud laughter,
you fail to realise the perils I've faced,
but you will begin to understand hereafter,
how my life's legacy was almost erased.

The echoes of my footsteps rang eerily,
foothold lost in a mountain of despair,
a trusted ally plotted my end craftily,
disguised in a veil of tender loving care,

My body was dashed onto a jagged rock,
do you hear the sound of broken bones,
as I entered a state of mental shock,
the wincing sound is partly of my groans.

Perhaps you view my cry with some scepticism,
may hap's you wish to taste the fruit of poison,
for sure that will lie to bed your criticism,
and surely enough you shall begin to see reason.

No matter I will continue to tell my story,
there will be those who hearken to my plight,
that love is not all sweetness and light,
for sometimes this feeling can be obfuscatory.

Painful Passions

Alas! These are my private tears shed
though I now reluctantly with you share
bare a wound cut deep, my life was bled
even now in torment, I speak with care

I once believed love was an existential fact,
the facts of love set me right my brother,
my so called beloved had my head cracked,
and suffered me with a whole lot of bother.

Love tore me to shreds like mince meat,
pity, pity! hung, drawn and quartered,
could not believe twas me in the hot seat,
a lamb before the altar to be slaughtered.

I tell you still scars in my heart remain,
a dreadful sense of weariness on my shoulders,
succour me oh mother! From this shearing pain,
and roll from me the weight of the boulders.

Once with me she loved with gusto, you see,
what caused her to now my demise seek,
her judgement so beastly in her pique,
though I'm incoherent, please bear with me

A Lament

She wanted from me an open relationship,
to satisfy the demands of her prurience,
so of to the new world she took a ship,
I still loved her despite this experience.

Then she transmogrified to a licentious whore,
philandering as if intoxicated by wine,
my demise will set her free she swore,
acting in outrage like a marauding swine.

She plotted that I be manacled in chains,
my love repaid with lashes of the whip,
and crowbars used to bash in my brains,
My heretofore love has forsaken me, I weep.

Seeking succour from the spirits of my forebears,
in supplication I prayed for the moment to pass,
imploring in obeisance, cheek stained with tears,
the deadly snake has crawled out of the grass.

How come I to love a harlot of Gomorrah
I gnash my teeth and rent my clothes in lament,
My soul burning in a conflagration of torment,
Lord plead I, surround me with your aura.

Blended Soul's Of Love

There's no one, I will rather be with than you.
Don't go telling me, my honest truth is a cliché,
I never promised to over throw the world in a coup,
so do not let my Honourable parlance fritter away.

Do not get me wrong, I could scale high mountains,
and brave the roughest weather since the tsunami,
but all I want is to sip of your love fountains,
not reveal skills superior to special force's army.

Will understand if you ask why I of you desire,
that is a fair question that deserves an answer,
Not a trap set to stumble on like a barbed wire,
so you can shoot me down like a Calvary lancer.

I like your splendiferousness, but not just that,
for there is something known as the oomph factor,
it is what makes a fruit bewitching to a fruit bat,
and sets off their affair like a nuclear reactor.

Thus I do not make empty promises if not intended,
for you to think I am a man that is most splendid,
hope with this simple words we are both transcended,
To a place from whence our souls as one is blended.

Twisting Vines

Will you allow me to cry with you today
so that tomorrow we can be happy together
Although now you may feel a sense of dismay
the tempest will blow away like bad weather

Do not beat yourself senseless with a cudgel
because you may have committed a silly mistake
whatever, I stand by you like a guardian angel
though around you there may be an earth quake

Listen, to stumble is part of a learning curve
please note the graph of life is never linear
along the way you must expect to bump and swerve
toughen yourself and face forward with good cheer

Maybe one day I will share with you my life story
I was brought down to my knees but rose up again
to appreciate the twining vines of the morning glory
now I toast each day with a glass of Champaign

and so my darling I cry you a rivulet of tears
I hope to share your burden and listen to your fears
only time will heal your strife till it disappears
but be reassured I'll be there for the coming years

The Square Root Of Love

I am trying to figure out a major conundrum,
that has bothered me a fair length of time,
it beats a migraine in my head like a drum,
what's the square root of love and is it a prime.

So can love be divided into multiple complexes,
tell me its main divisor that answers eternal,
find me the formulae that answers its paradoxes,
how can something so pure turn out to be infernal.

You see its fairly easy to find love these days,
School, work, clubs, if all fails there's the Internet,
yes, cyber space a place you can graze and appraise,
and set your love criteria in a synthetic word net.

If you're lucky to find love how do you keep it,
that is the calculation that presently defeats me,
interminable readjustments causing my brain to split,
I need to find the solution so my mind is set free.

Come put your heads to work, help a friend in need,
Do not stand there in a guffaw watching me bleed,
instead rush to find answers at your fullest speed,
for you will get a reward and that is guaranteed.

RECYCLED LOVE

Consider the possibility we're in love,
the words we profess are not just bombast,
we bring serenity like a peace dove,
despite times insolence we're steadfast.

Will a flower give nectar despite the sting,
spreading its pollen worth all the sacrifice,
or tempted for the pain to crush the bee's wing,
in the process watch gleefully its own demise?

Will you be by my side when the sunsets,
wait by the bank for the tides to recede,
wipe my brow with your clothes when I sweat,
and staunch my wounds whenever they bleed?

The mirror reluctant to reflect its image
hastily exposes grizzle in the crone's face,
but when it shatters there will by carnage,
collapsing from its lofty position of grace.

So when you say the word what do you mean,
all over me today and tomorrow you're gone,
as you recycle love with the next you spawn,
and you lies cause me to vent my spleen.

DINING ALONE

So here, dining all alone I am,
missing the times, we ate a meal,
the memories of value, like a gem,
recalling, how we used to feel.

Though I chew, gone is my taste,
my appetite with you, away went,
the love for you gone to waste,
and now it's too late to lament.

Time dimmed not, this felt hurt,
as betrayal in hunger gnaw,
pain ignored with my mind shut,
hoping in time the tone will thaw.

Vengeance for the lord a debt,
as my heart to time reconciled,
Heavens! I wish not to be upset,
Or forever I will be not reconciled.

My love for you still alive remains,
Though, I'm a cuckold for all to see,
but with my thoughts I remain free,
thine conscience weighted in chains.

Third degree Burn

Your words left me with third degree burns,
Scalding me deeply till I was in pain,
When I asked what has caused this turn,
You brushed me aside as if I was a stain.

I can see the White exposure of my bone,
That is how deep this wound has penetrated,
Made worse by the fire in your acerbic tone,
Like you meant to have my heart incinerated.

Now I lay low trying to nurse my deep wound,
Still at a loss if to you I am important,
Hoping that one day our destiny will be bound,
And we will be tied together by a love covenant.

How I long to wake up with you by my side,
To feel your body heat warm my heart and soul,
lifting my self esteem I become a man with pride,
for to entangle your virtue is now my goal.

Shower your Rose petals along my pathway,
for my feelings grow stronger by the day,
do not think for a minute I lead you astray,
for I want to be with you forever and a day.

My Love Not So Tame

Is my love tame that it touches you not,
but it glides like water off a ducks back,
my words to you having come to nought,
as if to your ears all I did was quack.

I will wrestle a bear with my bare hands,
then fetch you rare pearls from the oceans depth,
and search for the yeti in distant lands,
to prove my love to you I fear not death.

This love is priceless as the air I breath,
lovelier than all the jewels of the Nile,
more colourful than a Rose floral wreath,
for nothing compares to you by a mile.

Never you think my love to you is lame.
Never you turn my want into a game.

ODE TO JILTED LOVER

She arrested your eyes the way she stared
and charged your thoughts with confused emotions,
though you're not guilty for things you shared,
she sought to smear you with wicked intentions,
just like a criminal caught with loot,
she wanted to burden you with her guilt,
In multi colours of lies and false tears,
she claimed you are a brute,
and brought a stranger to the home you built,
pretending that she wished to calm her fears.

You are a prisoner of her conscience,
though your body is shackled your mind is free,
justice is not blinded by her affluence,
So do not from her opprobrium flee,
time is your ally in this foolish fight,
so wait patiently for every new twist,
from the figment of a mind raving mad,
wishing evil with spite,
to think its with the same lips you once kissed,
alas a love past has become so sad.

The wastrel made you climb a steep mountain,
and sought to have you thrown in a snakes pit,
because she wanted you to suffer pain,
until to her every whims you submit,
but the stripes in your flag are unblemished,
whilst her voice is croaked with phlegm and smoke,
and the stench of her ordure stinks like death,
she will be admonished,
for the sins she enshrouds under a cloak,
you seek for justice as long as you breath.

ODE TO A LOST SOUL

You blow your gasket for no real reason,
lost in the sad traumas of your childhood,
entrapped in this dark world filled with poison,
you feel your person is misunderstood.
it seems mammon has blinded your senses,
you fervently worship in it's altar,
and bow daily in its adulation,
then put up defences,
like a paranoid Hollywood film star,
if not feted in false adoration.

Your buzz is louder than a queen less bee,
lost in the dark hives of your deception,
you revel in your blindness with sad glee,
but you wallow in this misconception,
around you are hawks that see you as prey,
same as the sharks you surround yourself with,
but to them you are just a ready meal,
a full three course buffet,
you see they have fastened your soul with withes,
now they halter and stake thee lest you squeal.

You are pressing your self destruct button,
take a pause lest you blow yourself to hade's,
apply that break on your plunging piston,
desist from lobbing these verbal grenades,
do not curse the sweet fruit of your own womb,
by smearing it with dung from the pig sty,
for the stink will follow you a life time,
thereafter to your tomb,
too late you shall look to the sky and cry,
when you realise you're covered in slime.

ODE TO A MAN BREAKER

She stands aloof expecting compliments,
picture of cool, as she struts in a prance,
seen only, in her best accoutrements,
beware! She believes not in true romance,
smirking at the thought of such a concept,
the smitten throw love petals on her feet,
completely charmed into her deepest trance,
off their feet they are swept,
their souls lost in the moment of the heat,
to her every whim and caprice they dance.

Man breaker! You ring your heart in hard steel,
and cage your dark mind in irons of wrath,
smirking mirthlessly as their heart you steal,
piteously, they beg and fall on your path,
but although they cry blood you disapproved,
shaking your head in open derision,
no man can penetrate your harsh defence,
for you remain unmoved,
and repel the insects with precision,
with a lupine snarl show you took offence.

What exactly happened in your love past?
that like a pestilence you avoid it,
have you suffered from a trauma so vast?
You wish men thrown into a vipers pit,
as you reject them, their want increases,
and they wonder why your heart is stone cold,
they now know they have been left in the dark,
all hopes dashed to pieces,
just like humpity Dumpity of old,
they can never be together put back.

A Wild Raging Fire

Oh nubile princess! Across the blue seas,
you stir the lust of warm-blooded men,
till they wish to ravish you in their den,
instead they come pleading on their knees.

For warriors come to lay at your feet,
wishing your favour will fall upon them,
reduced to duties like your skirt to hem,
lest they hang from a rope on a cleat.

Their body controlled by your coquette ways,
as you philander like a vixen on heat,
outrageously dangling a sharp erect teat,
causing minds to be lost in a complex maze.

You eroticize even the prudish at heart,
that from frigidness they become lubricious,
and so much so, some become adulterous,
becoming zealous coverts on ways of the tart.

Nubile princess so whimsical and capricious,
men who fall in love end up as anxious,
But thou hath stirred a primitive amative desire,
that lights up in fools a wild raging fire.

Ode To Open Marriage

It used to be that marriage was exclusive,
a union of love between a couple,
but no more it is now all inclusive,
myriad of new partners in quintuple,
open relationships and swingers club,
these lovers in and out like lingerie,
no deference for a sacred culture,
that contract was a blurb,
past ways are a romantic reverie,
listen lest your mind linger in torture.

They scour the web for a brand new partner,
lustful models to attract bees to nectar,
you the spouse now left in the back burner,
as on their webcam they live and chatter,
you try to stop this at you own peril,
they are wise to you and steeped in deceit
until the day they call in their counsel,
it hits you, this is real,
you better wise up to the shameless cheat,
or you the cuckolded end in a cell.

Hail marriage! The harbinger to divorce,
that changes lives never to be the same,
fat lies are told with no hint of remorse,
tooled to play dirty it's part of the game,
some will smear their own wombs with poison seeds,
never mind the smell that will rank for life,
the purpose is a scorched earth policy,
Satan holds their life deeds,
he willingly stokes the embers of strife,
chilling your ex-spouse heart till it's icy.

ODE TO AYAYA'S DAUGHTER

To the goddess Venus a toast,
she offers a kid for your roast,
when her promiscuous appetite awoke,
she painted her lusty desire in smoke,
filled her vessel with brine,
and dined with a black swine,
then sought ways to garrotte her spouse,
as she scurried like a field mouse,
hawks hovered above her with mean sharp beaks,
for them she performed the drama of freaks.

Though her forebears left her lucre,
but her knowledge is mediocre,
she brought shame and dishonour to their name,
with the bitter fruit of her foolish game,
she smears her skin in muck,
and she quacks like a duck,
she has cried wolf many—A-times,
now alone she suffers her crimes,
the enemy was always in her camp,
squeezing her innards till she had a cramp.

What is her family if turn apart,
she has no clue,
insanity seized her soul from her heart,
her mind turned blue,
life fay with broken homes,
envious bile disgorged foams,
spat on her face till eyes became blind,
on a new partner ploughed,
seeds of a nimbus cloud,
it poured acid rain her madness pined,
buds of the petals yet to fully unfold,
but the scandal will be in full all told.

ODE TO AYAYA

Mighty god of thunder! Hail thee,
save your knight from a stout banshee,
who masquerades as a mother in law,
shield him from the poison of her death claw,
she laments a dark song,
sounding aloud her gong,
she seeks to kill love just like that,
with the stinging bite of a gnat,
gnarls of her lupine snarl haunting his sleep,
a bountiful feast of sorrow to weep.

She's madder than a mad hatter,
with no shadow of doubt fatter,
corpulence caused by too much indulgence,
matched by insufferable arrogance,
moods of a bi polar,
she screams in a holler,
and pretends to be of high birth,
until she is brought down to earth,
she waddles like a penguin with a huff,
to take a sniff from her sachet of snuff.

She came to witness the case of the knight,
sat in silence,
watched as her offspring lied he flew at night,
through her thick lens,
she muttered a dark spell,
sounding the knights death knell,
for the past when the knight resisted her,
she smacked her lips with crud,
tasting for his blue blood,
but the judgement for her was a blur,
her dark sacrifices has come to nought,
this was not the outcome that she had sought.

Your Milk Of Passion

You slashed unerringly at my feelings,
with the serrated edges of a cactus,
and garrotted my soul with an impetus,
a beast with no conscience in your dealings.

Your milk of passion caused a blistering burn,
that has corroded deeply into my affection,
I'm left to wonder, if this was your intention,
for you seem oblivious, you did me a bad turn,

My heart was plundered by the hate,
ripped, so I no longer felt its bleating,
and the loss of rhythm left me panting,
until I learnt how to accept my fate.

This was the legacy of love gone wrong,
though my eyes, now brimming with moisture,
but I will once again, recover my posture,
for as days turn to nights, I become strong.

Same sky that's goes grey in winter times,
soon blazes bright, when summer chimes,
although from me, your love was snatched,
but a brighter love, will soon be hatched.

No Regrets For Loving You

Loving you blind I offer not regret,
it is why my life to you was tendered,
for love was neither a chore nor a debt,
from which a high interest must be rendered.

That Salty water corroded the joist,
and the beams splintered from internal stress,
we lacked the foundation from which to hoist,
thus left to collapse under the duress.

Never cease I your epitome adore,
my love an estuary that flows to sea,
you alone can cajole me back inshore,
but otherwise from you I am set free.

If I be wrong thence love not worth the pain.
But perchance I am right we shall both reign.

The Wages Of Betrayal

Sometimes I feel lost in the sand of times,
much like a mighty whale beached by the shore,
wondering how it got to these strange climes,
lamenting the waves that washed it ashore.

I'm a castaway floating in my dreams,
wallowing in my state of self-pity,
as your affection drifts off with the streams,
my pain barely hidden in this ditty.

My antennae failed to pick the signals,
loving you had jammed my radars senseless,
just static noise was picked by my aerials,
I failed to sense that you are a temptress.

I'm ailed by the wages of betrayal,
I shall not repay by been disloyal

Love Reflections

In your eyes reflects rays of the sunshine,
though distance splits us, I feel your passion,
lush redolence, like the taste of port wine,
Oh! Shine your love on me with compassion.

Rest does elude me, till again we meet,
for your image visits my dreams at night,
I feel for you on your side of the sheets,
Oh! My fancy for you, with wings, takes flight.

Wild fires tore through the adore you once felt,
but my true love will always be steadfast,
for you have in my minds depth solely dwelt,
my good lord, lift the dead hand of the past.

From the ashes shall a new love arise.
One day I shall again stare in your eyes.

The Fruits Of Poison

She said her crops where pillaged by brute force,
ravaged by the marauding beasts with long horns,
each saddled tight on the rump of a horse,
and pierced her with fingers of jagged thorns.

The fruits ripened with humours of poison,
fertilised in swamps crawling with vipers,
which envenomed when it came to season,
her reason to punish her usurpers.

This execration offends natures laws,
a mother levied evil on her seed,
goaded by toxins of accursed in laws,
who wallow in the pestilence of greed.

She said she wad ravished by the conquest.
And so to her fruits she left this bequest.

Cleanse Thy Soul

Though, ye wrapped thyself with the finest silk,
thy mind is infested with crawling maggots,
and thy breast expresses stale and sour milk,
that is rejected by thy babies guts.

But thou art preen like a prancing peacock,
with pockets lined with shekels of silver,
singing to the rhymes of the crowing cock,
plotting in the ways of a deceiver.

What is the profit to thou that ye smirk?
Whilst thy name is soaked in piles of ordure,
and you're blinded by the gloom of thy murk,
until thy essence have become impure.

Thy fiendish ways leads thou to damnation.
Cleanse thy dark soul in rites of purgation.

Love Ended Too Soon

Recall the days of yore when love was young,
we lent the sun flames that kept it alight,
when we swung from twinkly stars and we sung,
of far flung lands in the trills of a Twite.

The time we used to lay blankets of clouds,
that rolled on vapours across rippled skies,
whilst in pleasure we purred with vibrant sounds,
till the wind whistled to match our love cries.

Now we can barely thread feet on water,
we traipse through the tedium of wistfulness,
but penance can still save the adulter,
from the pus that seeps from this abscess.

Do you recall when we bounced on the moon?
Do you recall what crashed this love so soon?

What Do I To See You Again?

Oh, what must I do to see you again?
should I capture the songs of a skylark,
and release it's tunes as petals of rain,
till the sweet melody sparks in the dark?

What if I hold a lion by it's mane?
with your name cultivate it's temperance,
if my love is false then let me be slain,
my faith lies in this power of romance.

I will heal the rifts that now plague this world,
calm the wild beast that lives inside of man,
if only you assure me with your word,
that I will forever be your yeoman.

When will my eyes feast on your personage?
Can I on your embodiment forage?

You Viewed My Love Askance

For past love you show nary a flicker,
your face as morbid as a rotten corpse,
that expired from too much imbibed liquor,
ending all chances to again relapse.

Whilst the glaciers melt, your heart is frozen,
emotions calved into rocks of icebergs,
in this sleet where you are a denizen,
your love has become settled in the dregs.

How could I engender so much hatred?
that you lay on bed of nails to hurt me?
and a mere thought of you fills me with dread,
by instinct, I search for a place to flee.

Your love transmogrified to repugnance.
Through a thick frost you viewed my love askance.

Let Us Take Flight

Let me smoothly touch down on your tarmac,
and taxi gently on to your concourse,
ready for my cargo to disembark,
as you feel the push of my vital force.

Do not be disturbed by the engine noise,
my fan belt may need some readjustment,
meanwhile you can enjoy some of my toys,
whilst I make the necessary adjustment.

Allow me to switch your mind to static,
till I can find the right radio signal,
to check if your weather is climatic,
with my new torsion, which is seminal.

Let our love concord take flight once again
Let us jet supersonic once again

Ashes Of Their Love

How much pain must they feel before it's gone,
though time flies the hurt seem slow to abate,
in this game whence they're but a helpless pawn,
for the love of a wench that has no rebate.

Their mind lies fallow in the wilderness,
punctuated by the tears of memories,
for the strumpets love they wait to harness,
better chance of them hunting for fairies.

They reach out at night to an empty space,
a forlorn attempt to recapture the past,
you can see the anguish lined in their face,
as in horror they reel with mind aghast.

Her wild fire scorched through acres of love.
She quenched her thirst with ashes of their love.

I Died To Be Born Again

My heart used to beat aloud like thunder,
but now drums an imperceptible ache,
for the way you cast my love asunder,
and left a trail of tears in your wake.

My eyes used to pop out balls of hailstones,
which has melted and left behind puddles,
as my cries were reduced to muffled groans,
I suffered the penance for your foibles.

My lips used to with love whisper your name,
now mumbles an incoherent babble,
for you turned my honour into fair game,
and with falsities you roused the rabble.

My arms which used to embrace you with zeal,
is now met with the cold draft of disdain,
and the chill has left them with a numb feel,
my overtures to you is all in vain.

Part of me died when you betrayed my faith,
but born again in the sundial of time,
if I never find a love so sublime,
I'm consoled I'll suffer no more love wraith.

The Stained Burros

I traipsed into the vaults of a deep dream,
wandering close to the cliff face of a cloud,
precariously to the edge of the ream,
whistling with a good cheer your name aloud.

My footing slipped so I grabbed at raindrops,
and sallied down to a mound of earth,
surrounded by stalks of colourful crops,
that dazzled me away from certain death.

A plant absorbed me into its main root,
then secreted me as a scent of passion,
till I floated to the scores from a flute,
weaving to the music of compassion.

You inhaled me deeply into your breath,
I became part of your serenity,
exhaled gently to encounter my fate,
to restore the poise of my dignity.

It was you who broke my fall from grace,
and stopped my descent to hell without trace,
you embossed my foe with the stamp of Cain,
and soaked the—critter like Burros—with stain.

I Can't Believe

When I think that mouth, used to love proclaim,
now rains down curses and abominations,
against them on whom she made a false claim,
aroused from the wiles of machinations.

That same voice that once used to sweetly sing,
is now rinsed in diatribes and invectives,
confabulations that where meant to singe
and stain the life and times of the natives.

Smell of lies that lures flies to excrement,
desecration of the ancient temples,
that those accosted fell down in torment,
through evil she gathers her disciples.

Thus the egg yolk was forced out from the core,
and the shell was shattered into pieces,
so that all who beheld gaped at the gore,
the sordid voyeur of discharged faeces.

Hard to believe this same mouth of love spoke,
now spear out sharp words into their eyes poke,
words that proselytise of the rapture,
can't believe she pushed them into pasture.

IS IT THIS LOVE?

Why fall in love when it leads to heartbreak?
you believe the pleasure is worth the risk,
and delve deep unconcerned if it is fake,
you fail to feel the sting of a thorns prick.

Think hard when you exult in this habit,
lest the pain of rejection wrings your heart,
like an abbot forced to wear a habit,
that was rendered to shreds by a church rat.

Now you sob and rent your clothes in despair,
and bath your skin in clouds of golden dust,
then gnash your teeth pulling tufts of your hair,
prize to pay for your veritable lust.

Yet your lover shows to you no pity,
but derives some pleasure from your sorrow,
while you search elsewhere for some empathy,
here love today, flown away tomorrow.

Why did you put your faith in someone else,
till your head starts to play tricks on your mind,
that you wish to backwards the clock wind,
refusing to believe it was all false?

Elegy To Truth

See those who skulk in the caves of falsehood,
indignation at the whiff of stale air,
fouled from effluvia that wafts from their brood,
but the winds blows right back into their lair.

They wish a father not to know his son,
with their impious ways smear the sacred bond,
and plant poison on the stalk of the corn,
till alas they wilt the shoot of the frond.

The idiots wag their tongues to mock the sun,
waiting for the rays itself to abscond,
but as they stare their eyes begin to burn,
still in their folly they fail to respond.

They buried the truth in a makeshift grave,
with a false epitaph on the tombstone,
here interred the bones of a galley slave,
who till death from his sins failed to atone.

All ye who see should lament with the scribe,
and harking not to the lure of their bribe,
for thou will be blessed in the ascension,
though ye may suffer now in thou dissension.

Laughter Eludes You

Laughter eludes you despite your wealth,
your mind ravaged with the madness of greed,
and disease invades your ovaries with stealth,
to squelch the wanton monster you breed.

Though you bath in milk perfumed with jasmine,
and supple your skin in lather of cream,
your pores leaks out steam from odorous spleen,
the toxins of mind that stings till you scream.

Still you wage a war of evil misdeeds
but you know not your enemy nor friend,
or appreciate the horror of your deeds,
your scythe cutting a swath until the end.

The serpent of doom is coiled in you heart,
tugging at your strings in a crawling mass,
till you wriggle like an amorous tart,
and your tongue waggles with speeches of sass.

Don't you know the rewards of your action,
are you too blind to see the reaction,
that suffers you in the midst of splendour,
though you still patronise the same vendor?

Privileged Pain

I feel privileged to have suffered this pain,
For, its an after effect of a love like no other,
although, it's all ended in a spot of bother,
if I had another chance I'll do it over again.

The finest blossoms must in the end wilt,
but what extravagant colours at their peak,
a fine display of accoutrements so sleek,
yet at the end the petals will start to tilt.

Sweet nectar, for which the honeybees land,
also attracts the attention of buzzing flies,
and if your affection turned out a pack of lies,
I am still the luckiest man for the glad hand.

Therefore to the memories I now doff my trilby,
glad for the fortuity of the happenstance,
I'm not bitter that love failed in this instance,
for, I'm of the belief that what will be, will be.

My ship in the expanse of the sea has set sail,
I cast my net wider in the hope I do not fail,
at least I know where the swirls are severe,
and the signs that I must for my anchor sever

My Beating Heart

If only I can show you now my beating heart,
you'll see your name scrawled in bold letters,
tightly admixed with your sweet love in fetters,
if only you can this beaten heart tease apart.

My heart surface embossed with a gold stamp,
of your insignia declaring my complete loyalty,
in me you'll find no modicum of disloyalty,
you alone light me up like an incandescent lamp.

it's your love signature that is my driving force,
without your consent my heart beats no more,
therefore I surrender myself to your adore,
till the twilight years as a matter of course.

So let me burden you daily with deep affection,
and with my body shield you from foul weather,
never in my thoughts will your needs be nether,
for you will not lack from my close attention.

If of my tintinnabulous heart you visualise,
and from this vision you can conceptualise,
that the concept of love is without logic,
then logically you'll not think me demagogic

The Falling Star

A star fell right on the edge of a fading moon,
became overcast in the ringlets of its shadow,
mourned the passing clouds like a dark widow,
laments the end of times that came too soon.

Marbles now lost it crashed down to earth,
swung in repose, as it's twinkly light faded,
upbraided by new realisms it became jaded,
a dearth of bosom friends, it felt like death.

Raised to it's feet once more by a rising sun,
it shot across the bow to scintillate brightly,
feeling the luminance of its sparkle sprightly,
once again rejuvenated for the long hard run.

Now it glistens as the northern most star,
a beacon of light to wipe away your sorrow,
harsh lessons today, but forward tomorrow,
think about this no matter who you are.

For, a star fell from it's perch in the sky,
from it's perch in the sky, it could not fly,
it could not fly, so it crashed down hard,
it crashed down hard, it's life was marred.

LOVE ON ITS HEAD

On it's head this love to which lies within,
the tingling crawls in the innards of my soul,
slowly guiding the rolling waves to begin,
choking the fervour, so as not to lose control.

An infestation that finds good dwellings,
in it's natural abode from whence it feeds,
on the nutrients to encourage the feelings,
that germinated from the implanted seeds.

Still I dipped my tongue on mulled red wine,
to taste the spice of uncharted territory,
an unquenchable thirst for which I pine,
yet the waters flowed from the tributary.

Despite the turbulence I'm in fine fettle,
at least the ballast is nailed to the mast,
comeuppance awaits when the dust settles,
the chastisement for wish, I break no fast.

Lo, the Wuthering gales of my roaring heart,
with sustained speeds off the scale chart,
criss cross the bodice of thy winsome self,
awaiting the flourish from thy inner self.

Her Secret Emotion

Has she found the secret of her soul energy?
she who swore never again love to fall for,
raves about the benefit of romance synergy,
a tender feeling she now wishes to explore.

See her heart now melting like molten lava,
from a simmering volcano that did explode,
gushing about her knight like excessive saliva,
as the embers of her skin from new love glowed.

Unravelling the synthesis of her quintessence,
the darkness fades away in the setting sun,
no more perplexed by the knot of her essence,
ready to let go like burst from a machine gun.

She no longer shrinks from her deep emotion,
creating a path in the thick brush of angst,
as she let's her desires to be set in motion,
preparing for the lucky one to come a long.

'Twas this secret that drew us together,
after the long search hither and thither,
but dare we mention the forbidden word,
lest the antithesis slashes with a sword.

Rambled Into A Crane

I ramble in the fields of my expressions,
skipping across rows of periwinkle hedges,
lavender blue florets sprinkled on wild edges,
transmitting colours to feed my digressions.

From the foliage she emerged as a sarus crane,
long legs only truncated at her shoulders,
length of her shadow cut across the boulders,
the glory of youth juxtaposed to a love swain.

Languidly she floated with the evening breeze,
the wind parting ways to give her passage,
blowing a frock decorated by a floral corsage,
on an embodiment of a demoiselle at ease.

She flashed me a smile of snowy pearls,
saluting me in a flawless posh accent,
as she walked by I inhaled her scent,
excitement causing me to spin in twirls.

I wait by the hedge for her to pass by,
hoping she can be my girl, I won't deny,
the girl that will make me love again,
praying I will not have to wait in vain.

Wishing On A Star

So many stars to choose from in the sky,
only you can twinkle my heart into a bow,
it is in your honour I now this kiss blow,
which takes flight to your perch up so high.

I reach forward to encounter your sparkle,
to rekindle the fire that still burns within,
but I become all frazzled by your dazzle,
tossed by the spool of a yoyo into a spin.

Please drizzle your sparklers over my substance,
let me winkle out the secret of your tinkle,
for your sprinkle will smoothen my wrinkle,
I'm enamoured by the cadence of your brilliance.

Watch me jump on the ellipses of your spheroid,
over the moon, to hang on your shimmering twigs,
then take me on a whirlwind tour of your digs,
through the pathway of the jealous asteroid.

I gaze upwards, wishing on a lonely star,
and before my eyes appears a superstar,
craning her neck like strutting Swans,
and it is for her favour my heart now fawns

Ephemeral Daydreams

Daydreams of a love on my shore berth,
as mist dissipates with vainglorious tides,
afloat across the ocean her motion glides,
awash with droplets of a euphoric rebirth.

The rustle of leaves whispers her name,
everyday that passes, ever closer is she,
gazing into the yonder atop a cherry tree,
my impatience for a glimpse of her frame.

I sniff the crisp air of a now sprung spring,
on proboscis alights elements of her scent,
a redolence of fresh lilacs, heaven sent,
the vibrant piquancy to which I cling.

Mesh of clouds forms into images ephemeral,
as the wisps of effulgent cirrocumulus hue,
a pictorial wonder, which in my mind imbue,
fantasies that sends my spirit on a spiral.

The plumes of her essence spews afloat,
for she is the damsel that rocks my boat,
from this reverie into my world come forth
and together we shall be one thenceforth.

I Once Loved

Listen let me thrill you with a tale,
don't you believe me that I loved once,
if I thrill you with a tale will you tell,
that once I loved, believe me this once?

Long tresses afloat in the air like a banner,
entangled in a mass of thick golden curls,
her almond face moulded into a stunner,
with those eyes sparkling bright pearls.

When she canters into my enfolding arms,
and melts into the warmth of my pores,
lips tasting of candy afresh a love farm,
a bountiful harvest we took on world tours.

I flew with the great eagles in the air,
gliding in the wingspan of her care,
and light as a single strand of hair,
that I tell you now this feeling was rare.

How come the lustre has lost its shine?
Grey tarnish deposits on a brass plate,
no pumice enough to polish the slate,
of a feeling that was once so fine.

A Smile So Sweet

The current of the stream so severe,
hopeless fool I am to try to wade across,
now must bear the burden of my cross,
and suffer my passion with good cheer.

Caught in a confluence of wind and sea,
trying hard to shield from the rogue wave,
I batten down the hatches to stay brave,
albeit in the end I was forced to flee.

For sucked into the maelstrom of a whirlpool,
blinded by the ferocity of it's vehemence,
a hostile aggressive force of belligerence,
did not expect an atmosphere so cruel.

How false an edifice built on quicksand,
the weight of love too mighty to support,
exposed to It's embrasure quick to contort,
guess it's time to shift this deceptive land.

You distracted me with your glitter,
then filled my lungs full with water,
trying to drown me in sea of deceit,
and all the time with a smile so sweet.

A Shredded Past

The lucid light brightens the moonless night,
Tinkling lustre composed of blinking stars,
soothe sun rays burst as the firefly stares,
but avoiding not the labour of it's plight.

Circle the journey which ends from its start,
even it meanders through troughs and mounds,
all roads leads to the places from it bounds,
If though with speed the strident may dart.

From the winds of times a new hope born,
dark pangs though fraught with chasms aloof,
leaps into the future to see who did goof,
and from the hill top the mindless is torn.

Shredded emergence from a lacerated past,
with it a foul weather laden with ill will,
an iciness that brings forth a bone chill,
the longer the impasse had cause to last.

With this in mind I expect no quid pro quo,
so I sit back reverting to the status quo,
watching carefully for when the mist will clear,
waiting patiently for something I most fear.

Dew Drops

Amour, when your affection for me took a flighty wander
I was in a state of disbelief my instinct was to resist
All attempts to keep the rudder on course were a blunder

The unit we built could not survive the clap of thunder
Buffeted by intense winds our lives crumbled, which was
Amour, when your affection for me took a flighty wander

Unbridled whispers determined our union was cast asunder
For even when I reached out in peaceful entreaties, I knew
All attempts to keep the rudder on course were a blunder

My head spun in crazy revolutions I almost buckled-under
The strain made me seek solace from amnesia, for I remember
Amour, when your affection for me took a flighty wander

Once my loyalty was used against me I had to knuckle-under
The betrayal memorized like hieroglyphics on papyrus, though
All attempts to keep the rudder on course were a blunder

Truly, I suffered most intense pain, this act was a plunder
As sediments of dew drops wearily on my eyelids settled, for
Amour, when your affection for me took a flighty wander
All attempts to keep the rudder on course were a blunder

If Only

If I had an opportunity to do it all over,
I will serenade you with my love every day,
melt you with affection like ice cream sorbet,
mesmerise you with my passion till you quiver.

Never will I be derelict to your necessities,
my attention will not waver for one second,
as your liegeman, all you need do is beckon,
I reckon I can now deal with your complexities.

I track the trajectory of your shooting star,
brighter than any meteor around the galaxy,
as your fireball shower dazzles the meta-galaxy,
Oh! Ignite the visible path of my falling star.

In this biting winds, it's your warmth I need,
coat me with several layers of your tenderness,
let me feel the analogue of your boundlessness,
this time I promise it will not be a misread.

My goodness! if only I could go back in time,
you will be astonished with a love so sublime,
and be beguiled by the synergy of my purpose,
never again will you have a need to be morose.

TELL YOU HOW I FEEL

Pardon, I write to you like this after we split,
there was no other way for me to reach you,
the last time we met you left in a hissy fit,
but I want you to know my point of view.

No doubt I can live, though your love without,
a rainbow arc bereft of its primary colours,
or a beautiful garden in the times of drought,
for what use will a ship be if its got no sailors.

Your smile, flashed past my peripheral vision,
landing on the unfolding of a flower bud,
and revealing the inner pulchritude I envision,
my heart jumped high and crashed with a thud.

I do not for you wile away my time pining,
though aloud my dreams speak your name,
constantly I wake up with my head spinning,
and it's to you my thoughts are set aflame.

Hope it's now essentially clear how I feel,
like a river bed that once flowed with water,
or a sweet lamb on it way to the slaughter,
essentially I hope this will at last be the seal.

CAN YOU SEE?

Can you see how I am short of breath?
My lungs fails to take in enough air,
snatching your love away not so fair,
I need you the way a plant needs earth.

The ripples of your thoughts line the streams,
blown away like footprints in a sand storm,
your twisting images dims in the waveform,
into the nomadic breeze as my love screams.

The last time my hands touched your face,
flowers bloomed in the fullness of summer,
but echoes of you faded before midsummer,
all that is now left for me is a blank space,

I listen to the winds for your love whistle,
and gaze at the clouds for any new sign,
maybe the stars will display your shine,
do not consider my words mere prattle.

Short of my breath can you now see?
My love as vast as the deep blue sea,
I travel with the whales in my search,
can you see my heart is your perch?

The Effects Of Our Actions

The nights travel to the years end,
taking my thoughts along the way,
a basic rule that guides me, my friend,
this I share with you, if I may.

Every action we on our journey take
may result in an intended effect,
this was the goal our mind set to make,
the desired outcome sought made perfect.

Then we have the flip side of the coin,
the unintended effect of our action,
that inadvertently our action purloin,
in totality it becomes a distraction.

Beware and bask not in a pyrrhic victory,
with no thought to the collateral damage,
when your exploits become contradictory,
and your victims are now on a rampage.

Please notice, I do not speak in a rage,
neither do I make claims to be a sage,
in this new future when I turn the page,
I outline the values with my actions gage.

HEAL THY LOVE

I wish its within my powers to heal thy love,
lance the boil that has infested your mind,
so you are free from this pestilence my love,
and together we both shall fly into the wind.

But a cancer has taking hold of your ardour,
spread its malignancies into your soul,
heretofore, cupid had wished to explore,
now even a miracle can this disease control.

Must I accept the death knell till senescence,
waiting cowardly for the harbinger's verdict,
the rest of my life bask, in my dreams evanescence,
locked up in a world of regrets like a convict.

But I prepare to search the seven seas for answers,
accepting you may well be long gone on my return,
although this risk may stab my heart with daggers,
onwards I journey like I have no worldly concern.

The search for everlasting love is not in vain,
along the narrow pathway will come a lot of pain,
but better that than a life lived on the fast lane,
for without love we are nothing but inhumane.

The Future of Yesterday

From the start thy gaze from the wondering eye met my stare
Cool perspiration ran swimmingly afloat the nape of my neck
Body temperature roused from cold depth to a feverish point
Seeking the warm comfort of reassurance I reached out beyond

Never knew this could be what hath sought ever so timelessly
Running amok amongst the ephemeral nature of nightly dreams
Tossing and turning amidst rapid eye movements of restlessness
Seeking the warm comfort of reassurance I reached out beyond

Thy debonair repose seemed the most perfect of the female form
Entrapped rhythmically every toss of a perfectly coiffed bouffant
Heartbeat protesting the very confinement in an inadequate aperture
Seeking the warm comfort of reassurance I reached out beyond

For the sage spoke about the past as a prologue for the very future
Beware my son for not everything that glitters is in essence gold
Scratch the surface and feel the weight to know thy true worth
Seeking the warm comfort of reassurance I reached out beyond

Wise words espoused promptly ignored in youthful exuberance
Swaggering confidently in the sure knowledge of invincibility
But then came the judgment of faithlessness please bear with me
Seeking the warm comfort of reassurance I reached out beyond

Verily the Betrayal by a chosen beloved most painfully inflicted
Rivers of raw emotion flowing freely from the ponderous wounds
Seven shekels from the king's purse cannot assuage thy conscience
Seeking the warm comfort of reassurance I reached out beyond

So much suffering to be subsequently borne in an enforced silence
The burden of unrequited love too heavy a load to withstand alone
From my cogitations musings are spoken aloud for the world thereon
Seeking the warm comfort of reassurance I reached out beyond

Cloak and Daggers

Cloak and daggers, thrust and parry
she seeks to inflict a deep wound
cannot relax for even one moment
no time to tarry awhile and ponder
keeping a watchful eye for the glint
the tell tale signs of a vicious swing
here it comes! here it comes! I duck
I must be alert to her wicked ways
therefore I am forced to murder sleep
lest I feel the stinging bite of her sword
how long will I be the aim of her scorn
as she relentlessly seeks for an opening
a weak moment to sink in the blade
directions, the nape of my jugular vein
hoping to drain away my life force
she fails again but she keeps on trying
what's going on she never gives up the fight
she must be possessed by angels from hell
I just cannot continue in this manner
neither can I surrender to her every whim
what am I to do about this, I pontificate
This is the dilemma that I face daily.

SOFT CHEESE

If I could gently hold your dainty hands,
clasp them tightly close to my body,
so that my fervour is inscribed into you,
as I boldly into your green eyes stare,
hypnotising you with the essence of my will,
and controlling the tempo of your emotions,
on this journey into the depth of your being,
in my search for the calm waters of bliss,
to trigger in you an affectionate disposition,
that will change the pattern of your pulse,
solely with the tender music of my breath,
till your chest swells with the pride of love,
and with endearment you whisper my sobriquet,
now every blade of grass becomes a Persian rug,
from whence we can frolic under the open skies,
watching the leaves dancing in the passing breeze
our bond cemented by golden rays of sunshine,
If only your dainty hands I could hold gently.

Remember These Words

Come back, let me water the Rose,
ready for the season of spring,
sprout me a beautiful bloom,
flourish in my tender care,
let the flush of your floret,
fascinate the fire of imagination,
your scent that perfumes the garden,
tickle the proboscis of true love,
the stem of your coquettish stalk,
swaying in the breeze with overtures,
set ablaze their lubricious dreams,
and en kindle a feeling unbecoming,
let your colours brighten the sunshine,
and reflect a powerful new fervour,
on those who are fortunate to behold,
let it be the talk of great wonders,
to those who go on staggering wanders,
it will be an incomparable, unconquerable,
and unbreakable edifice of world heritage,
truly of the highest universal standards,
remember these words, so they see?

THE SIGNS FROM A ROSE

It was a dreary cold winter evening,
my only company was my thoughts,
so I traipsed outside in reflection,
hoping to gain some Divine inspiration,
so there I was gazing at the grey sky,
not a single twinkle star in sight,
and the moon had gone on a wander,
but I could hear a rose faintly whisper,
beckoning me closer to keep the faith,
telling me if I had but a little patience,
her milk of benevolence will pour on me,
I will be blessed with transcendent wonders,
for the chilly winds will blow a kiss,
and the clouds will become deep blue,
reflecting the rays of the new sunshine,
forming patterns of deep red rose petals,
into a smiling face peering down at me,
showing me the signs of your true love,
telling me that you are in this for real,
and so with this signs I was reassured,
back to bed, my eyes shut in peaceful repose.

The Entrails Of A Rose

It suddenly rained rose petals in my purview,
strewn across the pathway in which I walked,
semblance of affection drizzling in plain view,
speaking the same language of which I talked,

Joyfully I stridently staggered in a swagger,
brimming with pride like a ruffled peacock,
please don't get me wrong I am not a bragger
who goes about espousing convoluted poppycock.

I actually saw the entrails of a Rose today,
a complex miasma of contradictions revealed,
as it divulged deep secrets long kept away,
and there at once the core was unconcealed,

Ah! You view my extispicy with your scepticism,
but wait until you see the flower by my side,
then go grind your teeth like you suffer bruxism,
for your scrofulous remarks are ever so snide.

This efflorescence will not wilt under my care,
I shall cherish it carefully this much I swear,
my solemn oath are not castle's built in the air,
with this gem I stand ready for the wear and tear.

An Inglorious End

Puddles of rain spattered at my feet,
as I travelled through memories lane,
into the receptacle of the debacle.
Painful re-enactment's refreshed anew,
bolted through every sinew within me,
jolt my senses into spasmodic distress.
I swooned in a paroxysm of my passion,
both hands stretched into a contracture,
my jaws clamped shut in a sardonic grin.
Slowly, I consciously took a deep breath,
regained control of my inner senses,
trying, to understand the reason why
the bulwark of our lives was vulnerable,
the rampart of our fortification so weak,
against those who always seek to destroy,
what they never suffered to build.
Felled the fine edifice of our lives,
but we must accept our part in the blame,
for like Nero we fiddled, while Rome burnt.
A most calamitous cavalcade of affairs,
hath brought nought but shame and vexation,
an inglorious end to a union of great promise
were do we go from here, as I wipe my feet?

ENTRAPMENT

Every time the wind blows a gale
scattering the falling autumnal leaves
racing down the road of perdition
my pulse kicks up a persistent storm.
For, twas this my first vision of you
standing over there like a gazelle,
just at the point of elopement,
then decided I was a friend not a foe,
you transpired to hypnotize me,
with a toss of your blond locks,
flirtatious eyes promising paradise.
Beckoning me towards your inner radius,
you spun an intricate web around me
I willingly allowed the entrapment.
Your attention commanded me with lullabies.
The power of your centripetal force overcame,
I swooned over in sweet surrender
and abandoned my guards to your every whim.
Alas! you slowly injected me with poison,
baring the fangs of your true intentions.
Paralysis of disbelief spread through me,
But then it was too late in the day,
For I was already blinded and deafened
and in love, I embraced you closer to me.
Until I was almost choked to my demise.
Realizing you were never good for me,
I swallowed the bitter taste of the antidote.
Slowly I can feel my soul recover,
There is life after all without you.

Dream Perfume

Right now I am badly aching for you,
wish I could feel you in my arms,
as we fall into a tight embrace,
I will greedily drink your body scent,
the one that wafts from your pores,
your sensational heavenly fragrance,
made from natures raw ingredients,
A blend of Juniper and eucalyptus,
sprinkled with a touch of Clary sage,
lightly crushed in cedar wood and cardamom,
with a hint of narcissus, oak moss and palm.

This secret formulae that is unique to you,
giving off an enticing and bewitching effect,
that offsets my neuro-chemical transactions,
altering my state of logical consciousness,
I become vulnerable to your enchanting spell,
as I am hypnotised into a deep trance,
I am powerless to whatever that you want,
you could excite, motivate or provoke me,
or you could use and abuse me whatever,
anything that may well tickle your fancy,
my future legacy is all in your hands,
this is the state of affairs as it is now,
but I sense the pervading presence of evil,
as I forcibly snap out of my dream state.

Opprobrium

Opprobrium, opprobrium why your love do I deserve
Ever you pursue my affection so relentlessly
Since the initiation of this debacle no rest
My every movement smeared by your deathly scent
Odoriferous stench to me like flies on detritus
What have I done that you vent your anger unto me
Dexterously I stoop and weave like a jabulani ball
My trajectory every way does not seem to elude you
It is clear that any hope for elopement is futile
I have thus to prepare myself for the inevitable
Knowing we must embrace at the fest of philistines
This warfare reluctantly waged to seek dissolution
Preliminary skirmishes commenced to test the resolve
With the sword of truth I join the thick of battle
Defend myself against hurtful and malicious fallacies
Deliberately peddled with no sense of moral turpitude
The Field of battle littered with deceit and betrayal
Raging fire threatens to consume all before its path
Memories of peaceful times a distant past be gone
But when it is all over will the fight worth it be—madam?

This Aren't No Love Letter

My dearest English Rose, I salute you,
I do hope you have recovered nicely,
from the sniffle ague that plagues you,
ever since my orbit sketched your form,
whilst you were out to do your shopping,
and I was then seeking some safe shelter,
from the foul humours of the bad weather,
when in a moment my chivalrous nature,
caused me to reach for your felled scarf,
our hands touched briefly, a moment in time,
but enough to spark an electrical firmament,
which is still burning deeply within me,
that I cannot tell the difference anymore,
between my want for you and my desire.

That was the day you wore that white dress,
indeed you enhanced the beauty of the garment,
looking like Cleopatra as a vestal virgin,
in the time of the great emperor Caesar,
Oh my Rose, for you only I join the legion,
march with pride to the land of upper Gaul,
and test my resolve when we face the enemy,
proving my mettle to you in full combat,
till I earn your trust and confidence,
I shall unsheathe the dagger in my scabbard,
and with the strength of my arm protect you,
bringing glory to all of your kingdom,
this I am swearing to you most solemnly,
as I genuflect to you in my declaration,
these words are not just another love letter,
for I wrote them only, as your humble servant.

Guilty As Charged.

Love was the heinous crime I was charged with,
made to face the dock in front of the jurors,
summarily ordered to give my evidence forthwith,
So I cleared my throat to expurgate my furore.

My lords and master's I am guilty as charged,
please hear me before you pronounce sentence,
in these circumstances I should be discharged,
expect me not to open the gates of repentance,

O! my love has changed something deeper within,
as though the mirror of myself has been broken,
a ponderous crack runs down the middle therein,
but the pieces still fit together as if unbroken.

If this now is a crime then I offer no defence,
Lords, if you will, banish me to the gates of Hades,
for I am proud to have committed this offence,
this is the simple truth which I hope persuades.

My lords "pro tempore" let me free on a love bail,
consider my attestation before sending me to jail,
if after your deliberation's you decide to impale,
I will still thank you for listening to my tale

GUILTY OF INNOCENCE

I heard loud knocks banging in my head,
the day l always feared has come at last,
my ears locked to the pummelling I heard,
this boom from the past was a mighty blast.

They have come in full force to seize my mind,
the day before she opened the channel,
to the table of love where we had dined,
and then forced me into a dark tunnel.

The weft of her thread was warped by the loom,
till the tension of the weave caused a tear,
and she left me to the prophets of doom,
to shield my damned soul through the gorge of fear.

They found me guilty of my innocence,
she tried to exchange my life for affluence.

PENAL SERVITUDE FOR YOUR LOVE

In penal servitude I serve for crimes,
committed when your heart I tried to steal,
as I look back to the beautiful times,
I stand ready to suffer this ordeal.

My desire for you never abated,
though I suffer a punitive labour,
I am not in anyway deflated
one day I sense you'll show your favour.

To your charms I am a recidivist,
waiting till you commute your resistance,
but consider me your love activist,
for whom my campaign will last the distance.

You see, this type of true love never dies.
I proclaim in a voice that never lies.

LIFE DETAINEE TO YOUR LOVE

I yearn to spice a morsel from your plate,
subsequently, cool my throat with your kiss,
you're like a drug that controls my heart rate,
the absence of which something is amiss.

Spin me with a crocodile roll around,
so I expire with your jaws clamped on me,
let my tomb become this hot pleasure ground,
in which I am now a life detainee.

Without you my life is bland like cardboard,
stale as sour bread encrusted with green mould,
exciting as gaping at a blackboard,
and off putting as catching a bad cold.

You own the copyrights to my love life,
with you the growth in my love life is rife.

DEBT OWED BE PAID!

She kissed him on his cheek and said goodbye,
but it was the sly smack of betrayal,
for he was marked out to be her fall guy,
cared little that he was always loyal.

Oh Nay! Ye hardened her heart as hard as stone,
till to the gallows she plotted his death,
then wanted his flesh skinned to the bone,
after he was departed from his breath.

The lord took pity on his wretched soul,
and listened to his plea for redemption,
saying come back to me my errant foal,
your faith has saved you from the accension.

Her thighs lusted for the phallus of sin,
Debt owed be paid for the wages of sin.

Dear Lord! I Dream Of Home

Lord! It seems faith against me conspired,
the woman I love has me rejected,
in your care my plight is now retired,
although I know I am not perfected.

Lord! She wishes to shackle me in chains,
have your poor servant thrown in a dungeon,
then an unmarked grave bury my remains,
quickly after she can my brain bludgeon.

Lord! I look forward to my freedom day,
watch the ship and sea gulls fight over scraps,
sitting in peace at the dock of the bay,
yearning for the places I saw in maps.

One day I shall be en route to my home.
I dream of sweet home, the scents of my home.

A Place Called Home

Every passing day I dream of my birth home,
the lapping of the beach wetting my feet,
and the swerve of surfers by no mean feat,
reminds me of the things I love about home.

A place where the time stays still waiting,
whenever I stand ready to wind the clock,
for a taste of fresh croissant from the block,
then off to the park for a day of skating.

The loud screech of a cockatoo screaming,
as I meander thru brushes on my jungle walk,
careful to avoid a cassowary on a sulk,
these memories that invade my thinking.

From the alpine heaths to the rain forests,
nowhere compares to the place I call home,
that's why my heart pines though I still roam,
for without home my soul will not rest.

Dreams of my birth home every passing day,
the evergreen eucalyptus trees swing away,
oh take me back home to my sweet home,
everyday I wake up dreaming of my home.

Your Whimsicality

Although I am besotted with your ambiance,
and try to pierce the haze surrounding you,
still you are conspicuous by your absence,
I sometimes wonder why all the hullabaloo.

Sights of you are blurred by colourful stars,
I only catch a brief glimpse of your shadow,
as you vanish into the sand dunes of mars,
Leaving me wondering if its all a foreshadow.

Whilst I wish my faith in you is justified,
the interest you show is not a passing fad,
and in the passage of time will be intensified,
your whimsicality drives me stark raving mad.

Hopes in me are raised of a timeless affair,
that will travel through the infinity of time,
with an intensity erupting as a solar flare,
and forever you shall be my partner in crime.

Let us crash the dishes surfing the life wave,
and take the risk for the things that we crave,
of course you are safe with me I am no knave,
I will be there for you till I go to my grave.

A Rose Set Me On Fire

and yet I still feel your shadows past,
the subtle fragrance of your aroma,
triggers your memory till I am aghast,
my escapism is to fall into coma.

Even so it is of you that I will dream,
garlanded as it were with rose petals,
but as I bath in your tidewater stream,
my reverie is shattered by your cymbals.

You know I stand ready to defend the realm,
bear arms with the sword of noble intentions,
forever in your service with you at the helm,
till you're ready to honour me with citations.

So you have no need to be so unapproachable,
to swivel and then swerve out of my reach,
stuttering, spluttering and then dissemble,
trying to confuse me with a figure of speech.

This love is a composite of want and desire,
you ignited the flames, now I am on fire,
do not live me in cinders and do a flier,
give me a chance, you will see I am no liar.

THE CURE TO MY HEARTACHE

What if I never from you again perceive,
you slipped away like you first appeared,
a freakish weather on a midsummer's eve,
that came with a force and then disappeared.

My thoughts will be engulfed in utter bedlam,
as I wonder what has brought about the truancy,
of the splendid lady who hath a natural glam,
and spoke the language of my soul with fluency.

As torrents of tears rain down my pallid cheeks,
I shall hence, will unspoken words to your heart,
my essence will travel by nature's telephoniques,
for I posses a key to your mind's navigational chart.

Wherever you happen to be you shall hear my call,
growing louder till you no longer can ignore,
the wailing from my spirit as pure as crystal,
that you begin to feel I am a man worth fighting for.

So I am dialling the digits that ring your psyche,
fingers moving with the speed of a love avalanche,
with you by my side I will again regain my panache,
and finally I will forever be cured of this heartache.

My Love Gate Is Open

What I've never known bothers me not,
the things I know makes up my experience,
a glimpse of your love makes a large blot,
I had to withdraw as a matter of expedience.

With a haughty mien you watched askance,
waiting with timing to spring your surprise,
once you vituperated I knew my stance,
it was not to tangle with a snake in disguise.

I failed to see the spots in your limpid eyes,
tongue laced in honey oh! A marvellous delight,
how wondrous your attention up in the skies,
a visage so winsome like a midsummer night.

Yesterday, I fear not that which I survived,
tomorrow with hopefulness for the unknown,
though I hurt now I hope it is short lived,
what seems a barrier may be a stepping-stone.

My love gate is open to welcome your carriage,
but I hope you leave your entourage behind,
the wind from them blows with an unsound mind,
to our boding affection they rather took umbrage.

THE CURE FOR LOST LOVE

The cure for a lost love is a new love,
though it might seem the soul is emptied,
and any attention—you are undeserving of,
you feel your ability to give has atrophied.

You alone know the potency of your anguish,
an excruciating pain like never before felt,
and in this sorrow you now wish to languish,
how was all lost—in retrospective you dwelt.

Your ever-present grief causes you to gallivant,
in your dream state you seek some satisfaction,
alas! the stupor of alcohol—is not enough adjuvant,
so desperately you search for a new distraction.

I repeat, the cure for a lost love, is love anew,
what you need is some fundamental interaction,
a sojourn into an introspective analytical review,
before succumbing to the lure of physical attraction.

No bother, if you call this rhetorical nonsense,
Say whatever comes to mind, I will take no offense,
for no doubt right now you are on the defence,
you may have lost the principles of commonsense.

Application For A Love Loan

I will need a love loan from your bank,
to tide me over in this period of drought,
so I come cap in hand to be bailed out,
my requests before you have drawn a blank.

I mis-invested too much of my warm heart,
on an attractive proposition with no solution,
leaving my reserves in a state of disillusion,
and all my sincere affection taken apart.

A short term credit with long term interest,
profit is well assured when my love overflows,
you cannot make a loss with what I propose,
I know you want to, though you feign disinterest.

Stay with me at this time of my love crunch,
and I will be with you thru rain or shine,
plus my name shall be first on your credit line,
come on now why don't you follow your hunch.

Ma'am let me secure this loan with my heart,
but if you may prefer any other body part,
and if you allow me to consolidate all my debt,
I make this vow in earnest to never forget.

Virtual World Friend

My phantom friend in the virtual world,
Since you first appeared on my reality,
my simple mind has done nought but whirled,
at the deep nature of your sensuality.

Everyday I look forward to our exchanges,
imagine you're the keyboard on my laptop,
so I caress every word with my phalanges,
maybe you do the same but with a desktop.

You have provided to me a perceptual stimulus,
for spatially I experience your telepresence,
as ultra filtered particles via glomeruli,
into this synthetic world, I feel your essence.

I am not even conversant with your appearance,
save the certitude you have a beautiful soul,
for your delicate words have shown a coherence,
that could not have emanated from a black hole.

Well maybe one day the virtual will become real,
when we meet we might both have such sex appeal,
and say wow! this could just be the real deal,
No matter, you will always find me a man genteel.

In Love With A Pixel

You know your mind is embroiled in deep trouble,
when against logic you fall in love with a pixel,
that you do not notice your chin grow stubble,
all day you stare at the boundaries of the bixel.

Though your stomach may thunder aloud like a lion,
you are too mesmerised to respond to any stimuli,
except that which grows ever stiffly in your loin,
transferred from messages captured by your oculi.

Everyone you know ask you to stop this nonsense,
wondering what had brought about this new madness,
that seems to have stole away your common sense,
and they shake their head in a state of sadness.

But you have done no harm to deserve this kerfuffle,
why is everyone getting their knickers in a twist,
it not like you get yourself involved in a scuffle,
neither do you go out daily to get yourself pissed.

Back again you go to check your favourite website,
you are not finished with this, not by a long sight,
as you hope the pixel who is for real in her own right,
emerges from your screen to squeal's of your delight.

Love By A Romantic

My Darling, meet me at the love junction,
as the light turns green I will be there,
we will leave behind all the commotion,
I'll whisk you somewhere with some calm air.

Let's take this journey into our affection,
to picnic at the fields of devotion eternal,
direct our thoughts from paths of inflection,
building a tight bond beyond the rational.

Together we will weave a story worth reciting,
a fairy tale across ages of magical folklore,
making the romance of love most exciting,
a shiny light for all new lovers to explore.

Our dedication shall resound the world around,
the exemplifier of what is a notional ideal,
an intellectual source for boffins to propound,
all trying to work out the basis of our deal.

The ascent into legends of mythical proportions,
must not allow us forget why in love we fell,
lest these giddy heights sound the death knell,
whereupon, the rarefied air has caused distortions.

LOVE CHATTER

I may well be to you a sentimental fool,
but my love for you is not for gimmickry,
neither is it perchance a handyman's tool,
to be cruelly utilised to mock with mimicry.

Be informed this feeling in not an erratum,
to be waved aside with nary a forethought,
but shall slowly gather pace to a momentum,
will not waver in changes often times fraught.

Flowers wilt in seasons but my love is constant,
so paste on my adore like brushstrokes of Monet,
and breath the still life of love in an instant,
before you a lush landscape with a blaring sun set.

Let the honour be mine to soothe your ache,
to hold your hands at a time of distress,
grant this at a time opportune for Gods sake,
so we share the burden for life's stress.

Darling, truly these words are my anthem,
I stand to affirm the testimony therein,
Of these sentiments I proclaim herein,
an affliction, you are my love exanthem.

TALKING LOVE

I do not mind you camping in my core centre,
pitching your tent wherever that you want,
you can take advantage of my amphitheatre,
please enjoy my generosity, have a croissant.

Now feel the intimacy of my decorous conduct,
let me clasp you with my natural passion,
then leave yourself open for me to deconstruct,
I will reveal to you, my love is in high fashion.

Steady on girl I have got vim for much more,
have a generous helping of me, its your choice,
please take all the time in the world to explore,
whenever you've had your fill you will rejoice.

Fan the embers of love with your harmonics,
let my sensations guide you to a high note,
memorise the phonics with these mnemonics,
as I take you speed jiving on my jolly boat.

You know I'm always ready for some action replay,
press the pause-play button if you want to resume,
then grapple with the strength of my sonic boom,
now I have the full license to your right of way.

LOVE PARLEY

A mere glance from you quickens my heart rate,
and it rebels in protest to be free,
so it can bite a morsel from your bait,
and with you indulge in a loving spree.

I preen all my feathers like a peacock,
stretch my legs like an eloping gazelle,
crow myself hoarse like a champion black cock,
because you're the one that rings my bell.

Although my love current, your embers fan,
you sway like a field of golden barley,
dusty from the dry winds of harmattan,
that my love to you feels like a parley.

I have not the will to resist your love.
I hope you feel the power of my love.

DREAM LOVE

It is your name I whisper in my sleep,
as you travel with me into my dreams,
and cause my imagination to leap,
I start to visualise you as bright beams.

I search for you in a cloud formation,
hope you drizzle on me with the rainfall,
soak me till you have my full attention,
and I have no doubt it is me you call.

Let us hang out by the lights of Neptune,
and count the eternal stars till they fade,
a log fire crackling will be our love tune,
we dance by the shadow of a moon shade.

How I pray that my dream will come alive.
It is your love that makes me feel alive.

CRAZY ENGLISH BIRD

What do you do with a crazy English bird?
Quaking all day long demanding attention,
a drama queen in a theatre of the absurd,
everything is met with condescension.

Well you must do your best to please her,
for she is the centre of the whole universe,
so do not get annoyed when she acts so demur,
or turns you in circles with her discourse.

You will need the heavenly virtue of patience,
coupled with a plentiful dose of forbearance,
to survive will be a test of your temperance,
some times towards her you will feel ambivalence.

but you must overcome this for she is sweet,
inside her, love overflows with an abundance,
she will lift you up when you are downbeat,
and you will benefit from her benevolence.

So I say, cherish the crazy English bird,
if she paints the air blue with a curse word,
do pretend that none of that ever occurred,
then she will transform into a real love bird.

ODE TO AN ENGLISH ROSE

Dark clouds overcast the sky on my walk,
to lift the spirits on a winters day,
and clear the cobwebs that cause me to sulk,
peace sought from the grind of a cities way,
the birds sang songs in coloratura,
door mouse darted about searching for food,
and the crows croaking out a strange warning,
a show of bravura,
that finally lifted me from my brood,
it was a perfectly tranquil morning.

When I spied some wild berries sprouting fruits,
tempted to harvest a bacciferous bunch,
but saw a fine visage new to these routes,
I waded through the thicket on a hunch,
lured closer by the sweet smelling fragrance,
to a bloom with a near recherché look,
it was the quintessential English Rose,
this encounter by chance,
silver pearls of dew drops adorned it's nook,
a most splendid blossom in perfect poise.

I reached out my hands to stoke it's petals,
excited by it's rare crimson colour,
I failed to see the red warning signals,
mesmerised by the bright lights of glamour,
did not notice it had a prickly thorn,
which pinched me with the sharp sting of a wasp,
injecting me with a passion for roses,
in pain my mind was torn,
and tossed in ringlets that left me agasp,
I wonder if I have lost my senses.

My Blooming Rose

My blooming Rose paints fine soulful murals,
fresco's made light with delicate shades,
of beach scene's, pale blue and lined with corals,
plus a divine mermaid with curled long braids.

Served by silkies, water nymphs and fairies,
a renaissance goddess from the ocean,
hath blown ashore across the seven seas,
setting a butterfly breeze in motion.

I stared in awe at this nubile princess,
as she serenaded me with love songs,
and offered me an exotic incense,
until my melted heart to her belongs.

She calms the tempest that deluges my sense.
She rules the storm waves with her commonsense

The Wisdom Of The Rose

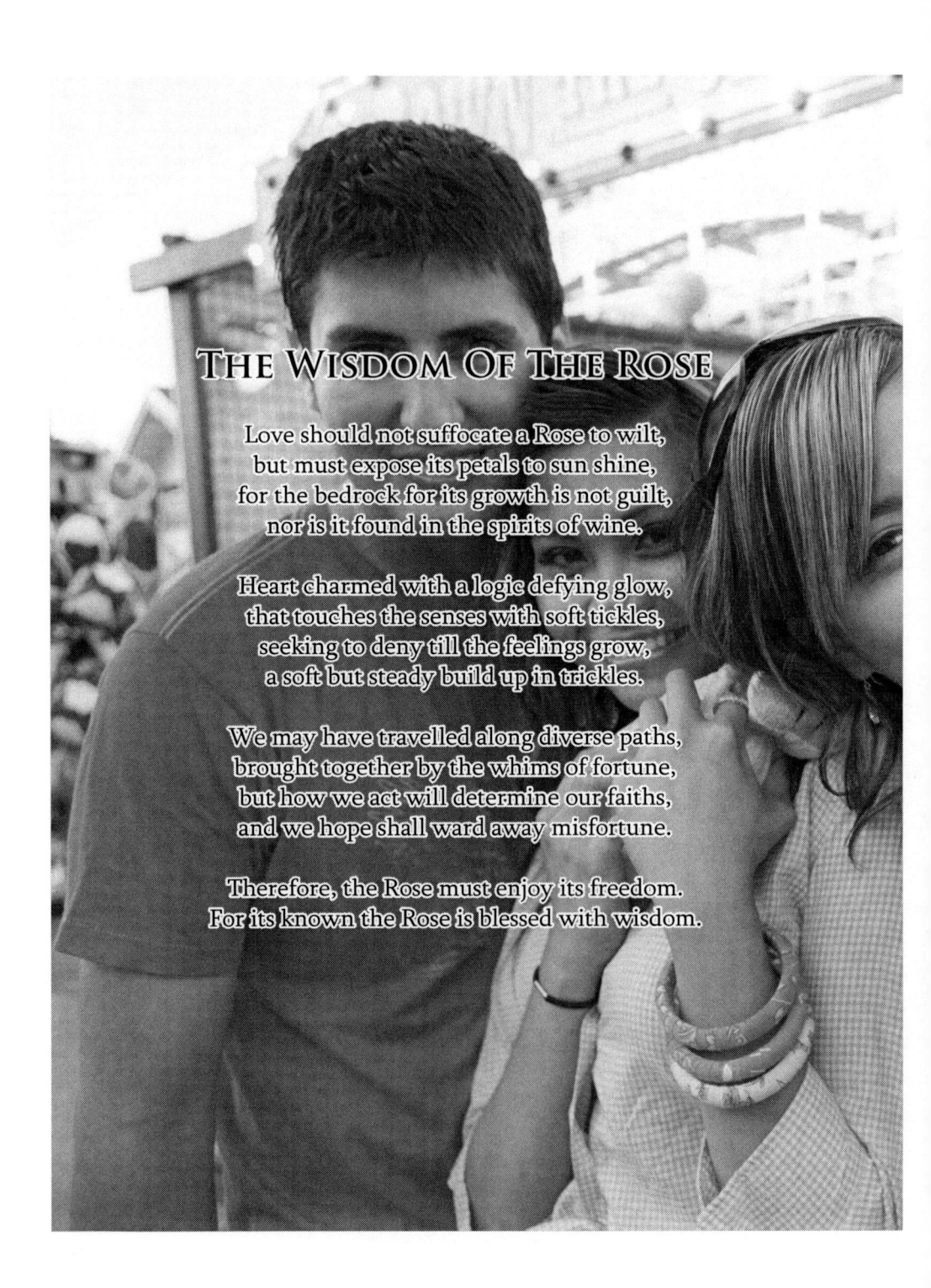

Love should not suffocate a Rose to wilt,
but must expose its petals to sun shine,
for the bedrock for its growth is not guilt,
nor is it found in the spirits of wine.

Heart charmed with a logic defying glow,
that touches the senses with soft tickles,
seeking to deny till the feelings grow,
a soft but steady build up in trickles.

We may have travelled along diverse paths,
brought together by the whims of fortune,
but how we act will determine our faiths,
and we hope shall ward away misfortune.

Therefore, the Rose must enjoy its freedom.
For its known the Rose is blessed with wisdom.

Unfolding Of A Rose Bud

I stood watch as your Rose buds unfolded,
your red petals emitting their fragrance,
the contours of your beauty well moulded,
and you shone with a luminous brilliance.

Your syrup invited wild bees afield,
some with poisonous stings that wilted your stalk,
though I tried to protect you with my shield,
I failed to see the swoop of the wild hawk.

My love was infected by the venom,
the spring was no longer safe to drink from,
and I possessed not the anti-venom,
I was forced to watch what you have become.

How this rancid air has stifled my breath.
I will never forget till comes my death

My Crimson Rose Butterfly

I saw you in a field of wild flower meadows,
distinct in a horizon of most special beauty,
the air decorated by a group of barn swallows,
and the buzzing bees carrying out their duty.

The plants displaying pearl coloured buttercups,
with your flapping purple wings in their sphere,
and me moving slightly forward to get a close up,
completing perfect scenery for an imaginer.

How I wish you to flutter on to my waiting arms
Let me feel the delicacy of your rare iridescence,
so I may enjoy the amorous nature of your charms,
as I bask in the afterglow of your efflorescence.

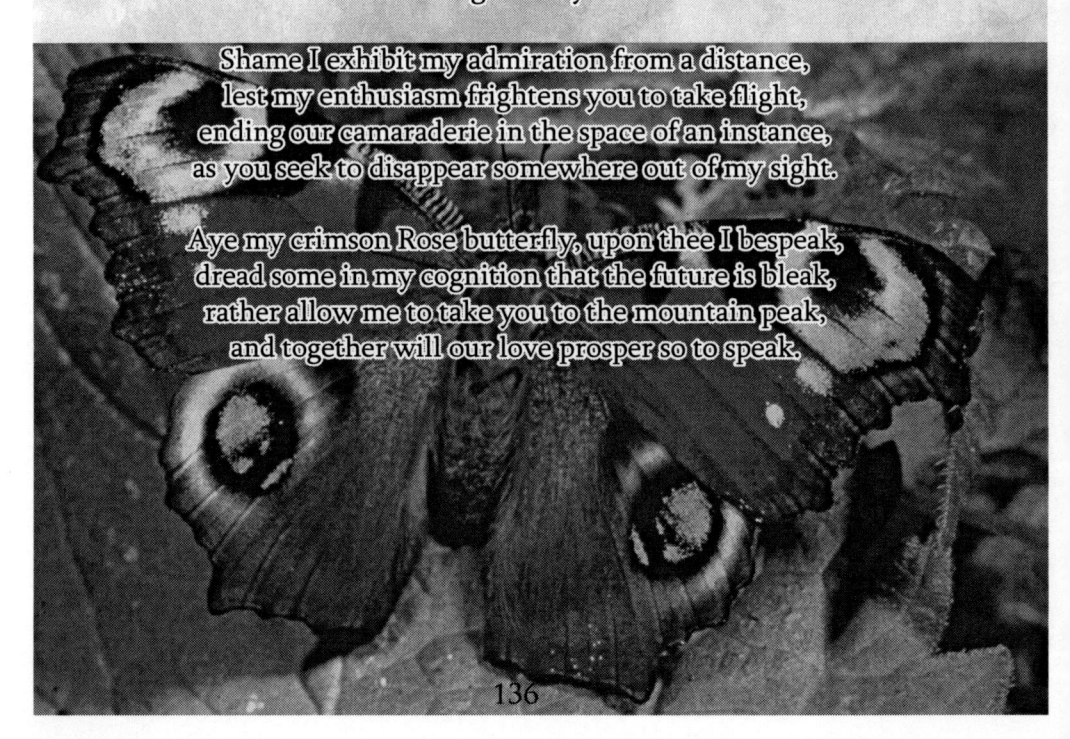

Shame I exhibit my admiration from a distance,
lest my enthusiasm frightens you to take flight,
ending our camaraderie in the space of an instance,
as you seek to disappear somewhere out of my sight.

Aye my crimson Rose butterfly, upon thee I bespeak,
dread some in my cognition that the future is bleak,
rather allow me to take you to the mountain peak,
and together will our love prosper so to speak.

Love Wings Like A Butterfly

If on my knees I anoint your feet with tears,
will you in return my true love have faith,
and wipe away my most abiding fears,
so that my deep doubts begin to abate.

Why do your wings flap like a butterfly,
and dance out of my reach when I am close,
just when I start to think your love draws nigh,
you vanish, to inflict on me new woes.

I need that love that sways the leaves to wave,
a brooding hen to cluck to its hatchling,
even if I become your galley slave,
or firmly attached to your apron string.

Although it may take more than a lifetime
I will fight for your love with my last dime.

Behold Thy Beauteous Self.

There used to be a time I felt my soul ebbing,
away from any feeling that could be termed love,
I eloped like a cheetah at any hint of its prompt,
living behind a puzzled puff of dust in my wake.

Loving felt like a glove that no longer fitted,
shrunk by the terrible facieses of past betrayal,
till I caught a glimpse of thy beauteous self,
the sight that accosted me so breathtaking.

I gasped at the discovery of the eight wonder,
and gaped at the enchanting vista that beheld me,
more spectacular than the display's of Aurora,
a magnetic field pulled me to your ionosphere.

You became the only centre of my attention,
invigorating me with the energy of your atmosphere,
now I cannot help myself but to ponder deeply,
if your heart is sturdier than the fleeting snow.

Will you blanket the mind with the force of an arctic blast,
and tighten your grip with the chill of your attention,
then melt away to reveal a deluge of bewilderment,
like glaciers in the aftermath of rise in temperatures,
once a new excitement passes your field of vision?

AHEM AHEM

Ahem ahem, excuse me for one brief moment,
I clear my throat to interest your attention,
but I lack the words to explain my intention,
so excuse me while I suffer this abashment.

Today you transported me into cloud nine,
as your vision descended on my embodiment,
I ascended into the nadir of your firmament,
by a gnawing hunger for you to be mine.

If only I could be the air that you breathe,
I will inflate my deep love into your lungs,
tickle your vocal cords, you speak in tongues,
till for this love you have a fullness of faith.

How I wish to be the tears in your eyes,
I will caress your cheeks when you cry,
moisturise your smooth skin as I glide by,
till your mood swings, right back to its highs.

My lack of dictum may fail to convince you,
if I failed to convince you to be my beau,
just because my syntax are all mangled,
I can only blame myself for I have bungled.

Simple Pleasures Of You

See the way the wind sways the palm trees,
so they toss their leaves in unbridled delight,
and marvel as the birds soar high in flight,
enjoying the flush feeling of the cool breeze.

Observe how the firefly lights up in joy,
on sighting the crepuscular glow of a mate,
sprucing it's keen wings whilst lying in wait,
but when he makes his advances she acts coy.

Cast your limpid eyes over the swirling waves,
and watch the way they twirl in simple pleasure,
rolling across the ocean span in their leisure,
whooping happily at the entrance of deep caves.

Relax as flowers unfold at a hint of the sun,
the bees rush to get the first taste of nectar,
sucking the pleasures into their juice collector,
to produce the honey you've in your sweet bun.

These wonderful images compare to your love not,
that weaves my emotions in a complex tight knot,
and I'm left gasping in my craving for some more,
hoping that you'll always remain my Cherie amour.

LETS KISS

Ready, steady, now purse your lips for a kiss,
allow me to buss them with my full breadth,
and you appraise the sweetness of my breath,
to take you faraway to the island of bliss.

Love that noise we make when we osculate,
those oohs and ahs with our eyes closed,
as the vermillion border becomes enclosed,
our melting cheeks begin to twist and rotate.

Let's drink from the springs of our fountains,
allow curios tongues the chance to explore,
as we conglomerate in this intimate rapport,
our mind soar across a range of mountains.

Dew drops settles on the water morning glory,
the moisture opens it's spiral bud in a tease,
same as we curl up tightly in a squeeze,
the pleasant spices of our blend so savoury.

Kiss me slowly, kiss me tenderly I'm all yours,
kiss me everywhere and in the out doors,
and with this affectionate kisses we woo,
to open up the petals of the heavenly blue

My Signature Over You

This is the true signature of my adore,
the way I sign into your love zone,
To authenticate this feeling my amour,
assurance's there's no falsities in my bone.

See the way I scrawl all over your zinger,
fancy strokes from my lashing bulb pen,
the swerve of my letters are a stinger,
you squeal with delight time and again.

I splatter you with the ink of my scribbles,
leaving unintelligible blots poodle,
till you get excited and start to nibble,
and find that you enjoy the taste of my doodle.

I switch from Verdana to Vivaldi no problem,
just tell my which writing style you prefer,
so I can scrawl down a motif of my emblem,
that your body was inscribed by a connoisseur.

So honey you are the cuneiform of my manuscript,
in bold letters I confess to be your conscript,
if you doubt me I will show you the transcript,
then maybe together we can write a postscript.

MILE HIGH CLUB

Girl take my hand, hold tightly don't let go
Feel the wind rush through your hair
Close your eyes shut, think about distant places
Let me be your pilot, take you on this journey
Navigating you to exotic destinations
Chill forget about the turbulence,
Do not entertain any fears
Am in control of the joystick, so relax
Put your trust in me, let me guide you through the trough
Now abandon yourself to the high altitude where I take you
Breath slowly, feel the thrust, the speed, the velocity
Do not hyperventilate, you may lose consciousness
As we defy gravity, lifting up to new heights
Arch back gently let me switch to cruise control
You have never been on a flight like this before
First class service all the way non stop we go
Champs and nibbles, whatever takes your fancy
Rushing through the clouds on latitude 69
The warmth travelling inside you spreads
Bring you to a smooth landing, no sweat
Glad you chose the first class cabin
Welcome to the mile high club

Social Idiot

I know you think I am a bastard,
but don't tell me I do not feel love,
I am a lover and I do love you,
just that my love tends to overflow,
like it is made to fill many cups,
when I am with you, I give you all my love,
just the way I do with the other women,
what do you mean that is not fair,
I don't get what you are trying to say,
are you saying I should give them half love,
Don't you think you are just selfish,
what you say you want for yourself,
you don't want it for other women,
does that even begin to make any sense to you,
I don't understand why you are so illogical
what do mean that I infuriate you,
you throw a cup of water at me and stomp off,
I will never get to understand what you're thinking,
which makes absolutely no sense to me,
or is there anything wrong in what I said,
I am shaking my head in complete confusion,
Maybe I am just too obtuse to get it,
okay if it makes you happy, its me
Just don't talk to me about love.

LIPSTICK ON CITY ROMANCE

In city romance love is no option,
but hides in the smudges of a lipstick,
that leaves a red stain but has no function,
you cannot wait to be rid of it quick.

Emotions weighty like too much baggage,
must be left behind lest rules are broken,
till the free bird is returned to it's cage,
were it can flap and twit away within.

There is no off load after a payload,
return to normal like nothing happened,
then get your system checked and hit the road,
next time your wits will be better sharpened.

Oh! This city pace consumed the romance.
To feel a heart is now a game of chance.

The Dearth Of Chivalry

What is romance devoid of any chivalry?
the time's you declare your full devotion,
virtue, courtly love and yes dare-devilry,
then serenade by expressing your emotion.

Readily, you nail your standard to the mast,
your feelings espoused with great eloquence,
trumpeting your love with poetry at full blast,
hoping with your effort they take cognisance.

You idealise with honour the lady you dreamt,
and you stand ready to be at their service,
of course by doing this you hope to prompt,
so she understands the basis of your premise.

I fear this courteous arm of romance is on the wane,
as anything you say can be easily misunderstood,
till you clasp your head tightly, like you are insane,
and stay rooted to the spot were you first stood.

This is why your metro sexual, is all but confused,
as these feminist have left them all bemused,
spinning them around like a yoyo, they are not amused,
and are all shadows of knights before, I have mused.

Dancing Orchid Of A Ballerina Girl

Ballerina girl you are an orchid inflorescence,
basking in the sunlight of a summers day,
though the wander of your gaze so far away,
I'm drawn to the glow of your luminescence.

The whorls of your sepals so distinctive,
as is your ripened labellum so engorged,
a legacy for which the gods so disgorged,
that belies pulchritude so instinctive.

When you resupinate like the dancing orchid,
you turn my world literally upside down,
as limbs peek through the slit of your gown,
my blood flows across the gradient of a rapid.

The delicate pedicle of your torso so slender,
enclosed in a narrow circle around my arms,
you're hypnotised by the wit of my charms,
hope you feel the fullness of my love is tender.

Dancing thaws the heart in a sea of emotions,
feeds the soul happy magic of a secret potion,
come riding along with me to a distant shore,
together let us around the wide world explore.

Flirting With The Moon

The moon batted it's eyelid at me today,
a coquettish flicker to set my heart ablaze,
drawing me in with a sensuous melodic praise,
to take me on a tour through the milky way.

It invited me to land on it's lunar shelf,
explore the beauty of it's rocky inclines,
promising it will send tingles down my spine,
all I had to do was to present my self.

Shimmering in livery of silver plumage,
it's aloofness cut a most regal figure,
crescentic repose of vivacious architecture,
I could not help but notice it's décolletage.

This promises to be a heady adventure,
a rush of sugar into a new space age,
I pumped up the levels on my pressure gauge,
to stock up my reserve for this risky venture.

So I said, hey moon I'll see you very soon,
if you croon for me I'll be there by noon,
you make me feel like a man born anew,
hope you never vanish from my field of view.

A Boast Of Love

Hold my hands, let's fly into the depth of space,
I will corral for you a constellation of stars,
and bring you fresh flowers from planet mars,
so we can make this new world our nesting place.

I'll crown you with the halo of my angel dust,
make you the great queen of all my galaxies,
and be the king to assuage all your anxieties,
a champion of your interest no matter the cost.

I will build you a castle with rock from Venus,
capture an asteroids for your use as transport,
fly you high to Neptune so you can hold court,
then to dine in the celestial sphere of Cygnus.

Your neck will be adorned with rays of sunshine
the wondering moon tamed for your merriment,
fires of shooting stars for your entertainment,
as I whisk you across the international date line.

These words are not just a grandiloquent boast,
and neither are they an extemporaneous riposte,
for you shall reign from the centre of my heart,
and together we will plot our full life's chart.

Reverse Exhibitionist

I want to heighten your experience of moi,
by fine etching of my graffiti all over ya,
motifs depicting my essence in the raw,
till you are left staring at me with awe.

I'll linger at the base of your five senses,
and trigger a riddle that provokes confusion,
combining words reactions like nuclear fusion,
you have no choice but to put up your defences.

You will be left scratching your head,
perplexed by the clues of the puzzle,
you are tempted to put me on a muzzle,
but to your wily moves I am far ahead.

Don't you realise I am a reverse exhibitionist,
stripping you naked with my words of colour,
until you are accusing me of a misdemeanour,
failing to glean the ways of an abstractionist.

See! You mooch on my word like a scrounger,
as you feed on my detritus like a scavenger,
but your ways have no effect on my swagger,
I continuously leave you dazed till you stagger

ODE TO THE MOON

Oh moon every night I gaze up to stare,
watching for the dark clouds as you emerge
I admire when you, all your beauty bare
that I long for our worlds apart to merge,
where is it that you go in the day time?
Do you visit a most secret lover?
Is that why you glow so brightly at night?
Tell me love is no crime,
to be now kept hidden undercover,
but should be in the open to shine bright.

Sometimes when my head is in a cloud,
I see you garlanded by silver stars,
to your timeless beauty my head is bowed,
no other can compare from here to mars,
when sometimes with me you play hide and seek,
darting in and out of dark clouds at will,
I have no choice but to dance to your tune,
you are a cheeky chic,
still you bend me by flirting with great skill,
that a mere hint of your sweet love, I swoon.

What is the deal between you and the sun?
I get jealous when you eclipse your lips?
Am I a voyeur watching you have fun?
I can't take my envious eyes off your hips;
don't you know that I can warm your heart more?
Give me a chance to be your special one,
let me feel the curve of your lunar shelf,
we will have great rapport,
more than you have with my rival the sun,
for ever you will be my saucy elf.

ODE TO A GIRL IN RED

You caught my attention with your dancing,
as you swayed about like an evening breeze,
every movement of your body fetching,
as you wriggled with laid back expertise,
the redness of your rose petals was dazzling,
your buds curved to the road of paradise,
promised by the flames leaping from your eyes,
your beauty was blinding,
I could not stop from casting the love dice,
if lady luck could help me win the prize.

What lucky man will have you in his arm,
my heart ached as I watched you twirl around,
my only bait was the wit of my charm,
with the glass spirits to guide how I sound,
I barked above the din of the music,
awaking the ground to come swallow me,
praise the gods your cracked a melodious smile,
your allure intrinsic,
like a well produced bottle of Chablis,
you oozed effortlessly with grace and style.

Thunder itself cannot keep me from you,
I will swim through shark infested waters,
to be the first suitor in your love queue,
then melt your lovely heart like hot butter,
once you taste my essence you will be trapped,
for I am made of rare honey and jam,
its yours to enjoy a generous spread,
all ready and gift wrapped,
for you will be my lamb and I your ram,
I am enamoured with you, girl in red.

MISS MOSSY GREEN EYES

She stared at me with mossy green eyes,
stones of emerald reflecting her thought,
that swayed like a pendulum in the skies,
pondering the answers that she sought.

The winds blew a gale as she wavered,
floating in the midst of nebulous clouds,
a tremulous thunk in her heart quavered,
then she expressed her doubts aloud.

She said, her erstwhile-lover was a scoundrel,
so her heart was now guarded by metal grills,
making sure she ended up not with a wastrel,
so I do not think she was looking for cheap thrills.

Is my path illuminated by a will o' the wisp,
pale flickers of rosiness quickly extinguished,
leaving my hopes dashed, I am left with a lisp,
for without her love my life is undistinguished.

Miss mossy green eyes, listen to my whisper,
do not depart from me, as if I am a leper,
me and you together are going to prosper,
so there is no need for you to ever whimper.

Doozy All Over Me

Aye doozy, you charm with your lips,
your every words leave's me to want,
I try to resist but my true love slips,
speaking your name daily in a chant.

Many times I wait for you to holler,
but my ears are open for a whisper,
you treat me as if I am a hustler,
I feel so dreadful that I whimper.

Heart twined with thicket's of barb wire,
as your captious self rips out my zeal,
my out stretched arms begin to tire,
I have to wonder why you're so puerile.

Never will I fail to wipe your tears,
but it's time that you take the lead,
chance for you to drive away your fears,
for I'll not leave your heart to bleed.

A passive love will fade out passively,
and an active love shall sprout massively,
but you show your ardour so impassively,
so please share your feelings more positively

Ode To Melancholy

You tried to be my best friend since divorce,
keeping close watch through the tribulations,
taking rein over my life with full force,
on you I vented all my frustrations,
still you embraced me in my solitude,
and took my hand as I suffered my grief,
you where a friend in need,
taught me to cope with a new attitude,
but my faith in you was a false belief,
you where soon plotting some evil misdeed.

I now see you where never a true friend,
you sought to control my yearning for life,
and wished me to always on you depend,
me think you are worse than my cheating wife,
with sharp steel prongs my mind was teased apart,
till stripped bare my skeleton was exposed,
but even then you seemed dissatisfied,
you travelled the dark path,
no rest until my flesh was decomposed,
for that you still will not be satisfied.

Melancholy, I cast you asunder
depart ye from the kingdom of my heart
I reject you with the force of thunder,
and bury you in the depth of the earth,
take heed for I now give you fair warning,
I will not fall for your amorous charms,
lift your insidious hands from my shoulders,
I will not be mourning,
neither for you will I sound the alarms,
gladdened when my mind roll off the boulders.

The Lure Of Melancholy

I sat in silence at the bench in the old park,
listening intently to the message from the birds,
remembering how you lulled me with empty words,
and then with my guards down fed me to sharks.

The groan of the train laden with passengers,
broke my reverie as my life flashed past,
the painful memory that left me aghast,
to the time I sought survival with foragers,

By Jove! Every day bygone I'm suffering,
the lure of melancholy seems so attractive,
but to succumb to its call is counter active,
therefore my mind answers by resisting.

Betwixt and between a blue and dark cloud,
I tiptoe carefully like a tight ropewalker,
avoiding the mellow voice of a sweet talker,
the future beckons with my head unbowed.

Remember when we kissed and our soul mingled,
when our lips touched and our hearts tingled,
when everything in the world was possible,
now the legacy this love left is impossible?

ODE TO BACCHUS

Bacchus you who make men forget their troubles,
and fine women to lose their good virtues,
even the coy can't remember their foibles,
for a time they leave behind their issues,
they chug copiously from bottles of wine,
their spirits are raised in your exultation,
through your venues they prowl on a pub crawl,
intoxicating swine,
see how you lift their expectation,
right until their words slow into a drawl.

Next day they wake up in a strangers bed,
lost to what took place in the previous night,
just like Lazarus woken from the dead,
they feel morose at the state of their plight,
as their head pound at the body insult,
they promise to avoid your future trap,
but they know not the power they deal with,
life sentence to your cult,
for without your influence they feel like crap,
any talk of cold turkey is a myth.

They salute and greet you lord and master,
and imbibe your habits to their life style,
as you preach to them like a drunk pastor,
you get them to do those things that are vile,
they lie in the gutter and heave their guts,
lost perspective of their social status,
as you start to take a toll on their health,
liver shrunk to peanuts,
all their life becomes stuck in a hiatus,
till finally they lose to you their wealth.

BETTER ME THAN THE BOOZE

You did rather be with me than in your party,
we both felt so good flirting with squiggles,
exchanging messages that made us feel hearty,
some of them so funny we ended up in giggles.

We both felt so good flirting with squiggles,
jotting down all kind of shapes and symbols
some of them so funny we ended up in giggles,
and we cared not if it made us look like fools.

Jotting down all kind of shapes and symbols,
we kind of just enjoyed each others company,
and we cared not if it made us look like fools,
for it seemed we had discovered an epiphany.

We kind of just enjoyed each others company,
exchanging messages that made us feel hearty,
for it seemed we had discovered an epiphany,
you did rather be with me than in your party.

Spring Burst Forth

The spring emerge from winters solitudes,
come forth, a fresh hope of blessings anew,
bounding greens promising new attitudes,
as we enjoy the sights of clouds pale blue.

Sunrise uplifts glorious spirits skywards,
when we watch curious saplings stare in awe,
they grow in confidence reaching upwards,
relishing the powers of divine law.

The streams swell with runoff of renewed pride,
chirping birds stop to drink from creeks and brooks,
a runner flashed past with long lopping stride,
and new lovers steal kisses on the cheeks.

Let the warmer climes burst out in full swing,
and meet me at the equinox of spring.

Reflections

For now I embark on a lonesome Journey,
taken the road that leads to my destiny.
The truth be told I fear for the tourney,
but determined to fall not into ignominy.

Along the way my reflections must reconcile,
synthesise my quintessence into components,
evaluating the different facets without resile,
this way am strengthened to face my opponents.

The environ I passed through left me beguiled,
Okay consider, when is a relationship exclusive?
you laugh thinking this conundrum is too mild,
until you find your exclusive affinity inclusive.

Now, you begin to understand the state of my mind.
Things are not that simple the way you had thought,
as we are all fighting against the prevailing wind,
hope you can settle your mind and not be overwrought.

So make no assumptions that am arrogant or conceited,
excepting you have suffered the pain of being cheated,
then you will journey with me so you are never defeated,
becoming wiser that the same failures are not repeated.

The First Time We Met

Though we met for the first time on Saturday
Your simple elegance caught my attention
We started a conversation like old friends
Dancing with each other through the night

Your simple elegance caught my attention
I could not resist the allure of your charm
Dancing with each other through the night
I have a feeling there is more to this dance

I could not resist the allure of your charm
You kept on smiling at me through the night
I have a feeling there is more to this dance
you gave me your number at the end of the night

You kept on smiling at me through the night
We started a conversation like old friends
You gave me your number at the end of the night
Though we met for the first time on Saturday

When We Finally Meet Again

Though I sent you a message hoping to meet for coffee
You made me wait for ages before you sent a reply
I heard you prefer to drink your coffee with toffee
So here I am trying to guess what it is that you imply

You made me wait for ages before you sent a reply
I recalled that you said the cinema sends you to sleep
So here I am trying to guess what it is that you imply
Maybe when we meet you want to discuss something deep

I recalled that you said the cinema sends you to sleep
How about we take a walk and talk mainly sweet nonsense
Maybe when we meet you want to discuss something deep
Whatever we decide why don't we let go of our defence

How about we take a walk and talk mainly sweet nonsense
I heard you prefer to drink your coffee with toffee
Whatever we decide why don't we let go of our defence
Though I sent you a message hoping to meet for coffee

We Meet At Last

You finally got your busy schedule free for the long promised date
I was determined to be on my best behaviour though nervous I felt
At the arranged time you called saying you will be fashionably late
But when you arrived my heart skipped a bit for you were so svelte

I was determined to be on my best behaviour though nervous I felt
What if there was no chemistry between us will you make an excuse
But when you arrived my heart skipped a bit for you were so svelte
And I flashed you my best smile and said why don't we go schmooze

What if there was no chemistry between us will you make an excuse
To the bar we went you had a light beer and I a big glass of white wine
And I flashed you my best smile and said why don't we go schmooze
Somehow you made me reveal all about myself right down to my spine

We had so much fun as the evening crept on we both laughed that
At the arranged time you called saying you will be fashionably late
When it was time to go I kissed you on the cheek and put on my hat
You finally got your busy schedule free for the long promised date

The Passion Of A Scribe

I profess to be a humbly craftsman,
the passion of a scribe make up my deeds,
though I may weave words like a bumbling swordsman,
they will still cut through evil and misdeeds.

My trade was learnt through the hardship of pain,
having trawled through the millstone of conceit,
when they tried to paint on my name a stain,
by spreading rumours of their loathsome deceit.

They put me on trial to face her demons,
bared talons and fangs sank deep in my flesh,
so as to redact the tract of my sermons,
I won't! Let them on the stake burn my flesh.

My letters are sharper than swords of steel.
they will never be able my mind steal.

Vainglory Of Rhymes

Some call me the great versifier,
because my verse test the fire,
as I release copious tract that inspire,
So don't go jouncing because you tire.

I am not a poet for you to lip sync,
for I spit out words to make you think,
then move to the next rhyme before you blink,
if you fail to recover you will just sink.

Never you shed a tear drop in my name,
because a verse I wrote seems to be tame,
for I did not come here to seek fame,
but rather to get my mind in a frame.

When you think you now know my weak point,
I will quickly wag my tongue and groove joint,
and leave you all in a state of disjoint,
taking you to the edge of your choke point.

You may wish to desist, insist but not resist,
for you know my rhymes will still persist,
without my words you struggle to subsist,
these words got you thinking, you reminisced.

Method Poetry In Character

I'm the appellation of whom I've spake,
swinging from the loupe of my rectitude's,
my self consciousness drives in the stake,
as inspiration accosts me with vicissitudes.

I delve into lands faraway and beyond,
battling with dragons from a realm anew,
and a sorcerer as he waved his magic wand,
trying my very best to find a breakthrough.

Virtual world merged seamlessly with reality,
words transpired with a maiden of my fantasy,
Is it real, is she real; I suffered her cruelty,
then retreated into my creations of ecstasy.

My art began to breath on its own accord,
it became a life out of my immediate control,
whenever I resist it slashes with a sword,
I'm left to deal with the deadness of my soul.

Therefore, I'm the persona of whom I write,
dancing with the wind of whatever may become,
the words are a shadow I cannot escape from,
but don't you dare take any pity to my plight.

Love Philosophy

It is achievable to attain what seems impossible,
limitation of mind may make it improbable,
so attack the conundrum with your self belief,
and the problem will begin to show some relief,

For there will inevitably arise a new dawn,
from whence a fresh beginning will spawn,
no matter how dark the present hour seems,
do not let the night strangulate your life dreams,

So chin up and take your medicine with pride,
soon you'll regain the length of your stride,
though you may have to swallow a bitter pill,
success will end at last how you used to feel.

The mirror reflects what hinders its pathway,
you're an image of your self-musings by day,
think positively and you manifest as such,
and negation of self, by thinking in as much.

I share with you the dynamics of my sapience,
twas these forethoughts lifted me off a black hole,
helping me regain a measure of self-control,
hoping you now take heed from my experience.

Oh Tree Almighty!

There stands the proud tree
Tall in its majestic girth
That all bow to its highness
Draped in its finest livery
from the top to bottom
Natures clothes finely cut
proudly it sways for attention
For all to see its beauty
Bristling in rude health
How the others are green with envy
Wishing they could but be a match
As it cast its mighty shadow
far as the eyes can see
No other can survive under
the harsh glare of its attention
it roots sink deep down in the soil
greedily sucking all nutrients
to itself no thought for anyone
Alas! the autumnal weather arrives
It leaves turn brown and is shed
Stripped naked like all the others
Looking forlorn with no friends
Oh! how are the mighty falling

TACTLESS CRITIC

Tactless critic who has to say something,
although what he has to say means nothing,
his sad life is bereft of any good fun,
and so he looks for someone to dump on.

His outlook has lost all things positive,
all he can see out there is negative,
he calls a bunch of apples, oranges,
and pen down nonsense to hide his rages,

He's a Pandora's box of paradoxes,
he has lost the bearing of his axes,
all he's got left is bombast and bluster,
and silly opinions he can muster.

He's really just a Grandiloquent fool,
waving his silly pen as a blunt tool,
nary a sign of social etiquette
manners absorbed from the social toilet.

Critique his work no matter how mild,
and he turns tail and sucks on his dummy,
same time crying for help from his mummy,
it turns out he is just a little child.

ODE TO A SON

My son, guess what it is me your papa,
how you have grown into a fine young man,
I recall you used to call me Tata,
now here you are calling your daddy Dan,
with a booming thunder of a bass voice,
every day I did not see you was lost,
I often wondered if you looked like me,
to leave was not my choice,
my departure from home was at great cost,
I always hoped that one day you will see.

I was with your mum the day you where born,
shook like a leaf blown by a stiff wind,
eyes brimming with tears from emotions torn,
my tough shell cast aside like a tree rind,
when I saw your milky skin and dark hair,
I vowed then to always be by your side,
and regret I could not keep my promise,
hope you know that I care,
my love was not washed away by the tide,
do not become a doubting Thomas.

My spirit flew to your side every day,
for you are my only begotten son
give your dada a hug please don't say nay,
from your eyes I can see the rising sun,
and I love you much like snow on glaciers
carelessly melted by global warming,
yet it transforms into a dam less flood,
not contained by barriers,
for it fans out like angry bees swarming,
nothing must come between me and my blood.

To A Daughter

Do you remember how we spent your birthday
how lovely it was to spend time together
we both watched a spider spinning a silky web
Daring any arthropod to cross its super highway
A butterfly displayed its waves of iridescence
Shimmering in the glow of a morning sunshine
Checked the deportment an angry praying mantis
Like a stance from ninja kung-fu master
Wondered what the slug worm do for a living
As one sauntered lazily past, no care in the world
Then a bumble bee buzzed our ear impatiently
Fetching the honey a hungry queen demanded
And that weaver bird twittering fleetingly aloud
Do you care to share a bite of my morsel with me
Ah and so we basked in each others company
Sharing the free offerings that nature composed
And with most delight shall educe this day forth
With the fondest of everlasting reminiscence
How we spent her second birthday together

Stroll Down Love Lane

Take a stroll with me down love lane,
the view perceived is a drop in the ocean,
as we wander thus, into a magnificent plane,
you will conceive the nature of my devotion.

My heart as stringent as that of a loyal swan,
once love struck, then enamoured a lifetime,
and we together, shall be entering a new dawn,
were you shall feel thereupon, love so sublime.

My constancy same as the clouds in the sky,
bringing you colours more than a rainbow display,
when I bestow on you a resplendence thereby,
you cannot help but flourish every which way.

You're the spark giving the stars their twinkle,
a magnet attracting constellation of galaxies,
o' copiously shower me with your love sprinkle,
I flatter not, you deserve all the eulogies.

Let me taste the benefit of your adoration,
so the exegesis of your devoutness is salience,
these words I have uttered are no contrivance,
but a clear measure of my deepest affection.

Who Will Tell Them

The voice of the murdered child in the street,
gunned down by the gangs of lost fathers,
their role models a fraternity of blood brothers,
taught in the school of life not to snitch.

The souls call from beyond the reasoned past,
bloody tears of a wasted generation amiss,
growing up with hisses and no male model to kiss,
never known a family to enjoy a repast.

Nobody told them things could be different,
no one guided them along the narrow path,
they saw was their parents torn apart,
in a divorce were nothing was abhorrent.

When will we tell them their reality is abnormal?
How many will be lost at the prime of youth?
Who will the angst of the displaced sooth?
Before society knows things are not normal.

This is a cry from the murdered child,
whose life was cut short like in the wild,
hearken now to these voices from beyond,
lest your kin is sent next to the beyond.

Dental phobia

They come to me repeatedly with a message of hate
I can see in their eyes they are petrified of this mission
For they shiver peering suspiciously while they await

How they seem to think it was I that caused their fate
Most would rather be somewhere flung from my domain
They come to me repeatedly with a message of hate

Well I try to reassure them the best way is to meditate
Nothing I say seem to bring to them any reassurance
For they shiver peering suspiciously while they await

The time finally comes when they have to concentrate
Just at that moment in time they become loquacious
They come to me repeatedly with a message of hate

Often matters can get worse when they feel me vibrate
But it is too late for them to flee, as they now lie supine
For they shiver peering suspiciously while they await

When it is all over they smile and tell me it was great
Next time I am still not sure what their mood will be as
They come to me repeatedly with a message of hate
For they shiver peering suspiciously while they await

A Knight Proposed

A medieval castle stood proud mindless to time,
as the flag of king George fluttered in the stiff breeze,
her aloof poise alluded to a laid back ease,
of beauty ethereal in a way most sublime.

An armed knight stood guard in front of the balustrade,
scanning the skyline from the slit of his visor,
on high alert to defend the house of Windsor,
stringent details causing his poor nerves to be frayed.

Catching site of her briefly in repose,
as she soaked the first rays of the sunshine,
he sent to her a courier pigeon to propose.

This was how to a princess a poor knight got through,
hoping to melt her sweet heart with his proposal,
till he wins her over he will this love pursue.

The Knight Decides His Fate

The moat around the castle was soaked with water,
muddied with the excesses from the castle drains,
and the detritus from the livestock remains,
after marching to the abattoir for slaughter.

In this dank morass his poniard between his teeth,
the knight reckoned life was not worth it without her,
he slipped into the dark mass with hardly a stir,
if her love heart to him destiny will bequeath.

All a knight want is to kneel at his ladies feet,
to worship her and then declare his loyalty,
that from his arms her enemies will know defeat.

This holy oath he has to his ancestors sworn,
to this love he was ready to give up everything,
for chivalry he was prepared since he was born.

A Knight States His Case

Although I'm but a pauper, true love has no price,
it's with this faith I for your heart make bold to bid,
to advance your service perform a great deed,
and hope that the bravery of my quest will suffice.

Your phlegmatic nature could calm the stormiest sea,
and sooth the mercurial tempers of a spring tide,
my heart will burst in colours if you are my bride,
and affirm my faith to the doubters so they see.

When you want for an oar I will bring you a ship,
ready to be the helmsman to steer your rudder,
and sail you across the wide world on a round trip.

It's for this reason a true knight, before you pleads,
resting on my knees ensconced deeply in your love,
hoping my honour attest, I'm a man of deeds.

The Knight Imprisoned By Love

I lie bound in this dungeon a love prisoner,
my compassion a flagon of prison made draught,
that deadens the sharp pain from the guards' weapons shaft,
providing the ache in my heart a dampener.

Although reduced to cleaning her privy chambers,
but my love undiminished grows in leaps and bounds,
even when suppressed by the lash always rebounds,
to the crest of her love my affection clambers.

I fear neither the iron maiden nor the rack,
no torture device man made can prise off my love,
though they may crack my back until it starts to wrack.

My love remains steadfast as the clouds in the sky,
as predictable as the setting of the sun,
and just as plentiful as my tears when I cry.

Testament Of The Knight

Am I sentenced to my death by the hang mans noose,
for daring to love above my station in life?
Like it's wrong to aspire for a home with a wife,
that I become a figure of fun to abuse.

I stand riddled with battle scars for my lady,
evidence my loyalty is beyond a doubt,
despite this I am treated like a common lout,
by she whom I most wanted to have my baby.

Let heaven judge me if my love was misguided,
I bemoan not one minute of my loving her,
no qualms whatsoever that our lives collided.

How poignant that my affection ended in strife,
but I stand proud to die with her name on my lips,
and refuse to renounce this love to save my life.

Knight & Damsel (I)

My sweet lady, let me genuflect,
your obedient servant greets you,
I waited as arranged yesterday,
by the enormous old oak tree,
close to the canal of hearts,
looking to hear your voice,
that settles a peace in me,
the day was still very young,
when I first arrived in hope,
darkness stole the daylight,
cockerels crowed to exhaustion,
the night owls had begun to stir,
still I waited to inhale your scent,
then cloud storms began to gather,
I was pelted with hailstones,
and struck by a giant thunderbolt.

For you where captured by a sorcerer,
the evil wizard of doubtful thoughts,
locked in a castle beyond the seas,
guarded by a frightful demon of fire,
only a true warrior with a clean mind,
with a heart of steel that knows no fear,
could rescue you from this lonely gulag,
I sheeted my poniard in my scabbard,
armed my self with the sword of truth,
to your service I flew with wings of love,
arriving to face a scene of devastation,
the land scorched for miles to the earth,
Bones of knights before accosted me.

My muscles glistened in the moonlight,
I unsheathed the sharp sword of truth,
with protection by the shield of honour,
I fearlessly joined the thick of battle,
a mighty conflagration was sent my way,
nimbly I parried this preliminary skirmish,
as I faced the monster demon sent by Amon,
He attacked me with a curved head cut,
I pirouetted delicately out of his reach,
feinted with a swooping wrist to head attack,
with a sweep cut the demon was vanquished,
that was how I rescued you from evils hand,
I was about to claim my long awaited kiss,
a bell sound restored me to consciousness,
with a message you could not make the date.

Knight & Damsel (II)

Bells rang menacingly across the hill top,
I could hear the chilling incantation of Amon,
In soliloquy he summoned the evil spirits,
beseeching them to answer his deathly cry,
the bowels of the earth groaned before me,
lips of giant flames sprang from nowhere.

Hearken to my call and bring back the sacrifice,
and the head of the knight who dared my powers,
the slayer of my loyal demon we mourn for him,
but I pronounce his demise must not be in vain,
rods of lightening shall strike down the knight.

We galloped furiously across the smoky plains,
my damsel strapped tightly across my back,
still groggy from the sedative effect of Eserine
my body ached all over from the hard journey,
saddle sore from the ferocity of the long ride,
guided by the lonely shadow of the moonlight.

A wake of vultures trailed our every movement,
Their neck scrawny as if they were half starved,
beady eyes peering hungrily at us in anticipation,
hoping to gorge on the entrails of our carcass,
the air was deathly still with an eerie silence,
this turned out to be the lull before the hurricane.

Suddenly a monstrous apparition stood in our path,
a gigantic ogre belching out plumes of sulphur
the air ranked with the putrid odour of it's breath
as it lumbered it's great frame across my way
a wave of it's hand knocked my horse into a stupor,
causing us to crash heavily to the ground.

With it's jaws it snapped the spine of my horse,
then turned to me with eyes blazing with odium,
gripping the nape of my neck and lifting me up,
he dashed my brains against the bark of a tree,
my consciousness travelled into the twilight zone,
as it dragged my body across tumulus mounds,
my damsel thrown like a rag across his shoulder.

As I emerged and departed from consciousness,
I could hear the morning bird make their calls,
the leering ogre brought his face close to me,
with all the effort from my fading strength,
I unsheathed my poniard and stuck it in his eyes,
he let out a gruesome bellow that shook the earth,
when I slashed my sword across his broadside,
causing him to scamper off like a puppy dog,
I had woken up from my dreams into a nightmare.

Knight & Damsel (III)

The morning broke through at last,
I could see rays of golden sunshine,
peeping occasionally through the clouds,
creatures of dawn began their daily task,
amorous frogs croaked their mating calls,
It seemed like a perfectly glorious day,
but I felt the pervading presence of evil.

My bones ached to the point of exhaustion,
every sinew of muscle in my body protesting,
a mighty head quake hammered persistently,
like a wood pecker suffering from OCD,
all I desired most now was a long rest,
but I knew we needed a safe shelter to hide,
to shield my damsel from the reach of Amon.

The vultures flapped their wings impatiently,
I summoned all the strength of my training,
invoking the spirits of my forefathers for help,
the damsel appeared to be in a state of delirium,
for she suddenly jerked forward in a stiff pose,
rigid fingers grasped my wrist in a vice like grip,
She seemed to suddenly posses a devilish strength,
I thought she was still delirious from the Eserine.

An alien voice suddenly rumbled within her,
she chanted as her body was invaded by Amon,
Oh ye knight who dared to defy my powers,
Ye have defiled the sanctified sacrifice of Amon,
I curse your forebears with a thousand pestilence,
Ye shall know never to again cross my boundaries,
I hereby decree that you're for ever encapsulated,
darkness shall descend and be your only light source,
slowly your skin will putrefy shearing from your body,
Ye shall be gladly embrace death to escape the pain,
I am not Amon the mighty if my words do not pass.

With these last words my damsel went limp,
and fell into my arms in a confused daze,
but this tranquil moment was short lived,
as I was whipped with force from her embrace,
a giant snake was wrapping it's coils around me,
slowly squeezing all the air out of my lungs,
and swallowed me in slow rhythmic contraction.

I was drenched with green slime from it's gut,
as darkness closed quickly as pronounced by Amon,
surely this time there was no avenue for escape,
desperate, I flailed out my arms to grasp for air,
my trusted sword must have tickled a nerve spot,
For the snaked suddenly heaved and regurgitated
disgorging it's green reeking vomit in a projectile,
I landed butt first in a mound of tall jungle grass,
there was my damsel cowering and quivering in fear,
It seems to me my nightmare only have just began.

Knight & Damsel (IV)

My body was as delicate as a dry twig,
I felt all my strength had been sapped,
in addition to all this I was famished,
stomach laid siege with a series of grumbles,
I needed nourishment to sustain my spirit.

The sun in it's beauty was relentless,
extracting every fluid from my battered body,
leaving me as parched as a desert island,
my thirst was worse than a dehydrated camel,
with tongue glued to the floor of my mouth
I urgently needed to drink and eat something.

My damsel must have sensed my sorry plight,
she made me comfortable in a bed of cut grass,
then off she went foraging for wild berries,
or any other delicacies this place offered,
reassuring me she would be back in a jiffy.

As soon as she left I tried to rest my mind,
happening to gaze into the distant horizon,
my senses was jolted alert by a Fata Morgana,
Phantasmal castles appeared floating in the air,
images transforming rapidly to reveal wonders.

An open fare with a bounteous feast,
exotic cuisine and vintage appellations,
my mouth watered despite my dehydration,
a femme fatale perfectly endowed beckoned,
dancing enticingly and wearing a leotard,
Her eyes, oh those eyes, mesmerised me,
promises of unbridled passion in paradise.

I threw all caution into the passing wind,
crawling quickly towards this wondrous vision,
unconsciousness must have overtaken me,
for next thing I knew I was startled awake,
by a sudden excruciating pain around my kidneys,
the vultures at last have lost all patience.

Sensing I was too weak to defend myself,
they had come forward to claim their meal,
squawking furiously when I shielded myself,
irritated at my every uncooperative movement,
the lead vulture attempted to pluck out my eyes,
on a signal the committee of scavengers attacked,
poking and prodding looking for a soft spot,
the dull thud of beaks on flesh could be heard,
causing a revolting sound with each new peck.

They would have torn me apart but for my damsel,
she arrived just in time to save her knights day,
screaming and shooing driving away the scavengers,
as it were my body was covered in multiple sores,
I seemed to have survived another dance with death,
but a heavy price is being exacted for my chivalry,
I must seek an urgent way out of this nightmare.

Knight & Damsel (V)

I was bruised, battered and covered in sores,
and Still Amon cast his evil shadow over me
every corner I turned there was opprobrium
I was lost in the slipstream of this nightmare
something decisive had to occur to end this
but for now I needed to find me some sleep
to rest my weary bones and recover my spirits.

My damsel tended to the sores as best she could,
I eagerly guzzled the coconut sap she offered me,
and hungrily quaffed the succulent fruit,
a replenishment of my depleted energy has begun,
she led me to a cave she discovered in her forays,
with great care we clambered into the cool den,
Kindly my damsel had prepared bedding of soft grass,
as soon as my head hit the grass it was lights out.

I know not how long I slept for,
or what had suddenly woke me up,
but something did not seem exactly right,
I could hear strange squeaky sounds,
what could that possibly be I wondered.

Yikes!! Rats as I saw the flaming red eyes
Not just ordinary rats, I mean giant monsters
Their long snout shaped in the form of trumpets
And they were fixedly staring eerily at us
I shook the damsel awake from her slumber
When she saw the hairy figures she promptly fainted
She was not going to be of any use for sure.

Quickly I made a fire torch from bunched straws
And used the flame to ward off the approaching rats
One brave one jumped over to nip a bite
With the back of my hand I thumped it one
Sending it flying, unconscious against the Walls
The closest rats to it pounced and tore it to shreds
cannibalistic hungry giant rats spelt trouble.

I bundled my fainted damsel on my shoulder,
beating a hasty retreat, seeking an escape,
the stinking creatures massed forward,
could I still be dreaming, it was hard to tell.

Knight & Damsel (V1)

It was difficult walking slowly in reverse,
For every step I took the monsters took two,
And they were getting bolder by the minute,
trailing my movement, waiting for an opening,
after what seemed an eternity I saw a light,
streaming from above an opening into the cave
at long last a way out of this entombment,
but my initial joy was only short lived.

That source of the light suddenly vanished,
now what new drama has Amon prepared for me,
my heart sank as I saw the wake of vultures
they seemed to have reinforced in numbers
as I watched them they swooped for the kill,
descending with the rapid speed of a raptor.

Meanwhile the rats where eager to confront us,
choosing that moment to launch their attack,
simultaneously about 3 dozen of them jumped at us,
just in time I glimpsed I small side opening,
No time to think I slipped in with the damsel,
but too late for my predators to apply the brakes,
their momentum causing them to crash into each other.

Neither the vultures nor the rats found it funny,
The rats snapped at the vultures with sharp fangs,
While the vultures tore at the rats with talons
then used their enormous beak to gouge out flesh,
I watched in horror at this fur and feather fight.

Large bits of flesh flew all over the place,
I saw the beak of a vulture tear a rat apart,
in one mad crazed swoop of it's bald head,
a chunk of red meat dangling from it's beak,
and a rat attached itself to a scrawny neck,
tearing open a blood vessel of the vulture,
Blood guzzled like a burst oil well in the glades,

Echoes of Squeaking and screeching resounded,
a terrible sound effect to the bloody spectacle,
The goriest thing I have suffered to witness.

Argh, the sight, the smell, the sound, disgusting!
excruciating even for a warrior like me to watch,
I could not remain within this chambers of horrors,
with difficulty I manoeuvred the damsel on my back,
through the narrow passage way into an inner chamber,
emerging into a labyrinthine cavern of natural beauty,
filled with crystalline stalagmites and stalactites.

However, this was no time to stand and stare idly,
I discovered a narrow tunnel out of this antechamber,
the damsel had at last recovered from her deep faint,
together we crawled painfully on our knees through,
Hoping against hope to find a way out into the open,
gradually we seemed to be going upwards on an incline,
after some hours we emerged into a cavernous space,
we could hear a whoosh sounds like fast flowing water,
which grew louder as we got closer to the source.

But we had disturbed a swarm of killer bees,
as they buzzed angrily out of their hives,
attacking us with multiple penetrating Stings,
In the panic i lost sight of my sweet damsel
falling blindly into the fast rushing stream
my life flashed before me as I cascaded with the flow,
the river must have flushed me back to the oak tree,
the place I was originally waiting for my date,
For I was woken up by the damsel tapping me,
looking as resplendent as a newly bloomed Rose,
not a scratch on her milky coloured epidermis,
asking with concern on her face if I was alright.

Lightning Source UK Ltd.
Milton Keynes UK
UKOW050432020212
186505UK00001B/177/P